# Financial Prediction
# using Neural Networks

# Financial Prediction
# using
# Neural Networks

Joseph S. Zirilli

INTERNATIONAL THOMSON COMPUTER PRESS
I(T)P ™ An International Thomson Publishing Company

London • Bonn • Johannesburg • Madrid • Melbourne • Mexico City • New York • Paris • Singapore
Tokyo • Toronto • Albany, NY • Belmont, CA • Boston, MA • Cincinnati, OH • Detroit, MI

**Financial Prediction using Neural Networks**

Copyright © 1997 Joseph S. Zirilli

I(T)P A division of International Thomson Publishing Inc.
The ITP logo is a trademark under licence

For more information, contact:

International Thomson Computer Press
Berkshire House
168–173 High Holborn
London WC1V 7AA
UK

International Thomson Computer Press
20 Park Plaza
Suite 1001
Boston, MA 02116
USA

Imprints of International Thomson Publishing

International Thomson Publishing GmbH
Königswinterer Straße 418
53227 Bonn
Germany

International Thomson Publishing Asia
60 Albert Street #15-01
Albert Complex
Singapore 189969

Thomas Nelson Australia
102 Dodds Street
South Melbourne, 3205
Victoria
Australia

International Thomson Publishing Japan
Hirakawacho Kyowa Building, 3F
2-2-1 Hirakawacho
Chiyoda-ku, 102 Tokyo
Japan

Nelson Canada
1120 Birchmount Road
Scarborough, Ontario
Canada M1K 5G4

International Thomson Editores
Seneca, 53
Colonia Polanco
11560 Mexico D. F. Mexico

International Thomson Publishing South Africa
PO Box 2459
Halfway House
1685 South Africa

International Thomson Publishing France
Tours Maine-Montparnasse
33 avenue du Maine
75755 Paris Cedex 15
France

*British Library Cataloguing-in-Publication Data*
A catalogue record for this book is available from the British Library

*Library of Congress Cataloging-in-Publication Data*
A catalog record for this book is available from the Library of Congress

First printed 1997

ISBN 1-85032-234-1

Typeset by Florencetype Ltd, Stoodleigh, Devon
Cover designed by Button Eventures
Printed in the UK by Clays Ltd, St Ives plc

# Contents

# Preface

Ever since there have been markets to trade, there have been speculators attempting to predict their direction. In this book, I will present a host of methods that will help you to predict the behavior of financial markets. These methods are all based on years of research into an exciting technique called *artificial neural networks*. An artificial neural network is an emulation of the neural networks in the human brain. I will show you how the brain's architecture is modeled by connecting artificial neurons into a matrix of neurons and how these neural networks can be taught to predict the future with surprising accuracy.

Two basic approaches to financial prediction are presented in this book: trend prediction and price prediction. The trend prediction approach is used to determine when the trend is going to change direction and the price prediction approach is used to determine what the price will be during a given time frame, normally the next day. Trend prediction is used for long-term analysis (weeks or months), whereas price prediction is used for short-term analysis (hours or days). A trend prediction net can be used to develop a **position trading** system. A price prediction net can be used to develop a **day trading** system. The terms position trading and day trading are used by speculators in the futures markets. Loosely defined, day trading is when a trade is opened and closed all in the same day, whereas position trading is when a trade is opened and held, possibly for many days or weeks, until it is determined that it is time to close the trade. Futures data was used to verify the techniques in this book, although any time series data such as stocks, stock indexes (Dow Jones Industrial Average), mutual funds, options, etc., can be used. I will also show you how to construct a *mechanical* trading system. A mechanical system is one that generates all of the information you need to trade a market. These systems will tell you when to buy and when to sell.

The real challenge in using neural networks for financial prediction is the construction not of the nets themselves, but rather of the transformations used to feed data into the net and the methods used to interpret the results that come out of the net. These methods will be described in great detail so that you can apply them to your financial prediction application. You will soon realize that this aspect of using neural nets for financial prediction, or for any application, is the key to success. In essence, you will be developing a good teacher for the net. Just like us, a neural net can learn if the information is presented in a format that is easy to comprehend.

The book is divided in four parts. Part One provides an introduction to all of the key areas necessary for understanding how to apply neural networks to financial prediction. This includes a review of neural networks, an introduction to the futures markets and technical analysis and a review of existing neural network literature related to financial prediction. Part Two details trend prediction techniques. A basic strategy for trend prediction containing all of the building blocks necessary to perform trend prediction with a multilayered, feed-forward neural net is presented. The entire process is explained using one basic technique in each of the various steps of the process and then other variations on this process are discussed. A clear, comprehensive description of what you need to develop a complete mechanical neural net system is presented. A discussion of why a mechanical system is important and the pitfalls of deviating from your system is presented. Part Three, price prediction strategies, is organized in a format similar to Part Two. Basic strategies are presented using a specific example, then a mechanical neural net system is presented, followed by other price prediction techniques. Part Four provides a starting point for further research by discussing how other branches of artificial intelligence can be integrated with neural nets to enhance your financial prediction strategies. Expert systems, fuzzy logic and genetic algorithms are discussed, and suggestions as to how they can be used in conjunction with other techniques presented in the book are presented. There are many hurdles, most very tedious, that one must overcome to develop a successful neural net-based trading system. One chapter assists the reader in taking those first steps and provides some pointers along the way. A short discussion of various areas that warrant further research is provided, as well as a summary and some general guidelines for moving forward.

# Acknowledgements

The writing of this book required the integration of two separate sets of disciplines. The first of these is artificial intelligence and neural networks. I would like to thank Dr Richard Mammone for his support and for introducing me to neural nets many years ago. Many of the methods and techniques presented were first developed under his guidance at Rutgers University. The second set of disciplines is market analysis and trading. I was first introduced to trading the futures market using technical analysis by Mr Pascal Mossa. Mr Mossa presented me with literature and expert training in all phases of trading and technical analysis, without which I could never have written this book.

My biggest supporter, by far, is my lovely wife, Gail. Thank you for your undying support and understanding and for the sacrifices you made throughout the writing of this book. To my children, Mary Grace and Joey, thank you for letting me use my computer once in a while. In memory of my parents, Joseph and Angeline, thank you for teaching me the value of a strong work ethic and for providing me with the resources to meet my goals.

# Part One

# Foundation for Financial Prediction Using Neural Networks

In recent years, researchers and developers, by using the back-propagation training algorithm, have been able to show that neural networks can be used to solve 'real-life' problems. One such real-life problem is financial prediction. Knowing when the stock market has reached its high or when interest rates have reached a low is obviously *extremely* valuable information. This book will show you that a neural network can be used to predict when a trend is going to change. Our financial markets have clearly demonstrated through the years that they trend in cycles. The timing of the tops and bottom of these cycles has been studied time and time again. This book takes a fresh look at this problem, with the application of neural networks.

Part One provides the foundation for the remainder of the book. The background necessary for the comprehension of the techniques presented is provided in this section.

# 1
# Review of neural networks

Researchers, in hopes of achieving human-like performance from computers, developed the concept of the **artificial neuron** (Lupo, 1989). The artificial neuron emulates what we know about how the neurons in the human brain work. These simple neurons can then be connected into a complex network, whereby the **synapses** of one are connected to others and the relative strength and weakness of these connections can be modified. The process of modifying these connections based on some external stimulus is how the neural net learns.

Neural networks consist of a large number of very simple neuron-like processing elements (artificial neurons) linked together by a large number of weighted connections that encode the net's knowledge (Lippmann, 1987). This architecture lends itself to a parallel processing environment with distributed control. Many of the neurons can process their information independently of others, although there are some critical dependencies that prevent a totally parallel implementation. The emphasis of neural networks is on automatically learning the internal representations (weights). Two classes of training methods are used to determine the optimum weights of a net: supervised and unsupervised. The core difference between supervised and unsupervised learning is that a supervised learning algorithm requires a desired solution to be known a priori, whereas an unsupervised training algorithm does not. A supervised training algorithm will normally begin learning by setting all of the weights to random values and then will iteratively modify the weights until the desired solution is achieved. Unsupervised training algorithms allow the neurons to compete with each other until winners emerge. The resulting values of the neurons determine the class to which a particular data set belongs.

## 1.1 The perceptron

The basic building block of a neural network is the perceptron, or artificial neuron. Here an artificial neural network will be viewed as a structure that imitates the human brain's interconnected system of neurons. The components of the brain are either replaced by hardware elements, such as transistors and resistors, or simulated using software. Electric signals

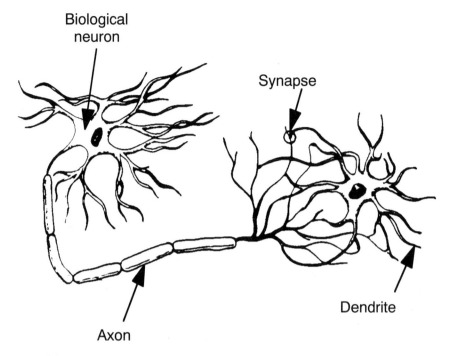

**Figure** 1.1 *Biological neuron. The human brain has $10^{11}$ neurons and $10^{14}$ synapses. (Lupo, 1989. © 1989 IEEE)*

passed between neurons are either inhibited or enhanced, depending upon what the neural network has learned, similar to the way in which the brain's neurons pass on electrochemical signals. In order to describe the elements of a perceptron, I will first describe a biological neuron and then show how its components are replaced by artificial equivalents.

A biological neuron, as depicted in Figure 1.1, has the following key elements:

- the **soma**, or nerve cell, which is the large round central body of the neuron (5–100 microns thick);
- the **axon**, attached to the soma, which is electrically active and produces the pulse that is emitted by the neuron; and
- the **dendrites**, which are electrically passive and which receive inputs from other neurons by means of a specialized contact called a synapse.

These three elements are simulated in an artificial neuron, as depicted in Figure 1.2. The soma is simulated by a summation element, the axon is simulated by an activation function and the dendrites are simulated by weighting the inputs to the perceptron. The perceptron sums $N$ weighted inputs and passes the result through a function called a **non-linearity** or

Weights

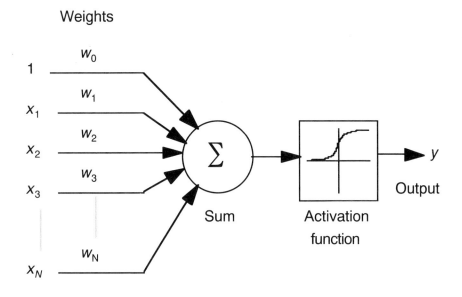

Inputs

**Figure** 1.2 *Artificial neuron.*

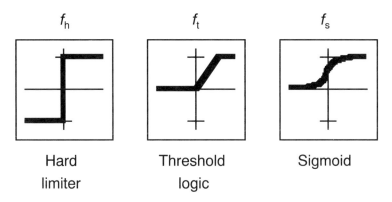

**Figure** 1.3 *Three types of non-linearities.*

**activation function.** The perceptron can be characterized by an internal threshold or offset and by the type of non-linearity. There are three common types of non-linearities, as depicted in Figure 1.3: hard limiter non-linearities, threshold logic non-linearities and sigmoid non-linearities.

This approach takes the knowledge we have of our neurons and simulates it with the mathematical model in Equation 1.1.

$$y = f\left(\sum_{i=0}^{N} x_i \, w_i\right) \tag{1.1}$$

In this equation, $x_i$ is the inputs, $y$ is the output, $w_i$ is the weights and $N$ is the number of inputs. Note that we sum from 0 to $N$. $x_0$ is called the *bias* and is set to 1, whereas $x_1$ through $x_N$ provide the actual inputs to the neuron. The bias input is therefore driven by $w_0$, which gives the neuron an added capability, independent of the inputs. This input derives its name from the fact that it can bias the neuron toward a particular level.

To obtain the results in this book, the sigmoid non-linearity given by Equation 1.2 was used. The sigmoid non-linearity is a requirement of the back-propagation algorithm, which will be discussed later.

$$\frac{1}{1+e^{-\Sigma}} \tag{1.2}$$

Each perceptron has the ability to learn and recognize simple patterns. For example, a perceptron can decide whether an input belongs to one of two classes, as shown in Figure 1.4.

A single line can be learned by the perceptron that discriminates between the two classes. The learning algorithm has the responsibility of modifying the weights, such that the desired output is achieved. The perceptron is trained by presenting it with a set of inputs $(x)$ and recording the output $(y)$. Based on the error between $y$ and the desired output $(d)$, the weights are modified as to reduce the error. One of the first techniques used to adapt the weights was called the perceptron convergence procedure (PCP). The PCP algorithm is as follows:

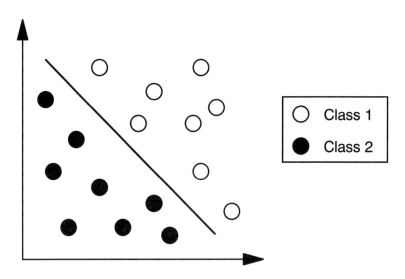

**Figure 1.4** *Perceptron classification.*

*Step 1:*   *Initialize weights and thresholds*
Set $w_i$ $(0 \leqslant i \leqslant N)$ to small random variables, where $w_i$ is the weight from input $i$.

*Step 2:*   *Present new inputs and desired outputs*
Present new continuous valued inputs $x_i$ $(0 \leqslant i \leqslant N)$ along with the desired output $d$. Note that $x_0 = 1$.

*Step 3:*   *Calculate actual output (Equation 1.3)*

$$y = f_h \left( \sum_{i=0}^{N} x_i \, w_i \right) \tag{1.3}$$

*Step 4:*   *Adapt weights (Equation 1.4)*
where $\eta$ is the rate at which learning will take place $(0 \leqslant \eta \leqslant 1)$ and $d$ is the desired correct output.

$$w_i = w_i x_i \eta (d - y) \tag{1.4}$$

This procedure is repeated until the error $(d - y)$ reaches an acceptable level, ideally zero. The perceptron was very interesting when first discovered but was soon abandoned when it was proved that it could not solve the simple exclusive OR (XOR) problem (Figure 1.5). Two distinct lines are required to classify properly the four states of an XOR. As the perceptron can learn only one line, it cannot solve this simple problem!

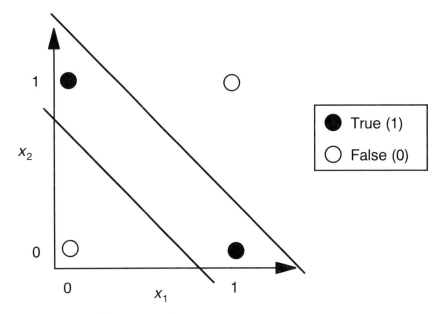

**Figure 1.5** *Exclusive OR solution.*

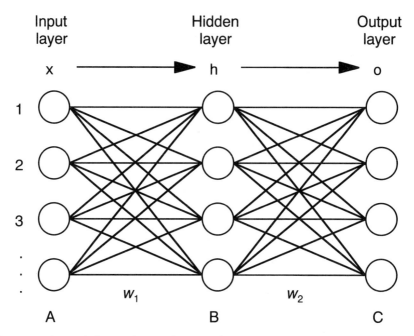

**Figure 1.6** *Feed-forward neural network.*

## 1.2 Multilayer perceptrons

It was then discovered that if these perceptrons were linked together, output to input, in a network, problems (such as the XOR) that require multiple decision boundaries can be solved. These networks, called **multilayer perceptrons**, are what is commonly referred to as neural networks. This approach seemed to be an elegant solution, but researchers soon learned that the simple PCP algorithm for training was no longer sufficient. This was due to the training problem with **hidden layers**. An example of a multilayer perceptron with hidden layers, also called a **feed-forward neural network**, is shown in Figure 1.6.

A hidden layer is a group of nodes whose inputs and outputs are only connected to other nodes, not an input or an output of the network. When this occurs, the PCP algorithm fails as the desired output of a node in a hidden layer is unknown. A solution to the hidden layer problem is the **back-propagation** training algorithm.

## 1.3 The back-propagation training algorithm

The back-propagation (BP) training algorithm is used to adapt the weights such that the net's outputs approach and, ideally, equal the desired outputs

(Rumelhart *et al.*, 1986; McClelland and Rumelhart, 1988; Knight, 1990; Carpenter and Hoffman, 1995). This is accomplished by determining the difference between the actual and desired outputs and applying that difference to the weights that were used to determine it. Before the BP algorithm can be described, a better definition of layers and the terminology used to describe them is required.

Neural nets are constructed by connecting groups of perceptrons (layers) as follows:

**Input layer:**      Provides external input to the network.

**Hidden layer(s):**  Receives inputs from the input layer or another hidden layer and provides inputs to the output layer or the next hidden layer.

**Output layer:**    Receives inputs from a hidden layer and produces the outputs of the net.

The output of each node is called an **activation**. Inputs are presented to the input layer and activations flow from the input layer, to the first hidden layer, to each successive hidden layer, to the output layer and finally out of the network (Figure 1.6).

The remainder of this book will use the notations as used in Figure 1.6 (Knight, 1990). Neural net notations vary significantly in the literature available on the topic. I have found the following notations to be the most logical for a neural net with one hidden layer:

$x_i$    The output of input unit $i$ (note that the input layer is simply the values presented to the net)

$h_i$    The output of hidden unit $i$

$o_i/y_i$  The output of output unit $i$

$d_i$    The desired output of unit $i$

$w_{1ij}$  The weight from the $i$th input unit to the $j$th hidden unit

$w_{2ij}$  The weight from the $i$th hidden unit to the $j$th output unit

$A$    The number of units in the input layer

$B$    The number of units in the hidden layer

$C$    The number of units in the output layer

$e_{1i}$   The error generated by the $i$th hidden unit

$e_{2i}$   The error generated by the $i$th output unit

$\eta$    The learning rate

Note that the notations in the previous sections were slightly different in that they used notation that is more commonly used in engineering and computer science literature.

We saw that when using the PCP training algorithm, each unit's weights were adapted independently of the weights for all of the other units. When training units in the hidden layers, the desired output is unknown. But we do know the desired and actual outputs for the output

**Table 1.1** Input/target pairs (patterns) example

| Inputs | | Targets |
| --- | --- | --- |
| $x_1$ | $x_2$ | $x_1$ XOR $x_2$ |
| 0 | 0 | 0 |
| 0 | 1 | 1 |
| 1 | 0 | 1 |
| 1 | 1 | 0 |

layer, so we can calculate the error at each output unit, and propagate it back through each hidden unit, adjusting its weight so as to minimize the error.

Before a neural net can be trained with the BP algorithm it must meet some basic constraints. The net must be fully connected and layered, whereby each node is connected to every node in the preceding and succeeding layers. The net must also be feed-forward only. All activation must flow only from the input layer to the output layer. There can be no connections back to a preceding layer. The BP algorithm also requires a sigmoid activation function (Equation 1.2) and input/target pairs (Table 1.1).

Once all of these constraints are met, the BP algorithm can be performed. The input/target pairs (also called **patterns**) are very important as they represent the knowledge that the neural net must absorb. The patterns are analogous to a teacher's lesson plans. The input patterns are the questions that the teacher wants the students to learn, whereas the target patterns are the answers to the questions. The student is obviously the neural net in this analogy! The teacher asks the questions, and if the student gives a wrong answer the teacher tries to tell the student where he or she went wrong. If this scenario is repeated often enough, the student will eventually give the correct answer and the training will be completed. Also, the questions must be given in a sequential or random order as opposed to leaning the answer to one question at a time. Otherwise, the student (like the neural net) will forget the answer to the first question by the time the last one is learned. A net must be presented with all of the patterns at once and be allowed to step through each pattern until the total error accumulated from all the patterns is sufficiently low.

Enough of analogies, now let us see how the BP algorithm trains a net. Two passes are required for each pattern:

*Pass 1:   Forward pass*
        Present inputs and let the activations flow until they reach the
        output layer.

*Pass 2:*  *Backward pass*
Compute error estimates for each output unit by comparing the actual output (pass 1) with the target output then use these error estimates to adjust the weights in the hidden layer and the errors from the hidden layer to adjust the input layer.

The key is to estimate the desired output of each hidden unit, thereby providing a desired output on which the error of the hidden units can be based. The is done by summing the error calculated at the output layer and multiplying it by the output layer's weights (Equation 1.5).

$$d_j = \sum_{i=1}^{C} e2_j \, w2_{ji} \quad j = 1 \dots B \qquad (1.5)$$

where $d_j$ is the desired output of hidden neuron $j$.

Each time a pattern is presented to the net, a complete forward and backward pass is performed and the error at each output neuron is calculated ($e2$). The sum of these errors is called the pattern sum of the squares (pss) and is given by Equation 1.6.

$$\text{pss}_i = \sum_{j=1}^{C} e2(i)_j^{\,2} \qquad (1.6)$$

where $e2(i)_j$ is the error for pattern $i$ at output neuron $j$. The pss is summed over all $N$ patterns available to give the total sum of the squares (tss) as given by Equation 1.7.

$$\text{tss} = \sum_{j=1}^{N} \text{pss}_i \qquad (1.7)$$

This whole process is repeated many times. Each time the complete set of patterns is presented to the net, one **epoch** is completed. An epoch is defined as one complete pass through all available patterns. The tss will continue to decrease as the actual outputs get closer and closer to the desired outputs. At some point, the outputs will be close enough. This closeness is measured by tss. Training is considered to be complete when tss is less than some acceptable level. Appendix A provides the complete details of the back-propagation training algorithm for those readers who would like to implement their own neural net.

Many epochs are usually required, even for simple problems. For example, the XOR problem requires over 200 epochs to train only five units and nine weights. Once you have trained your first neural net you will have a good feel for the limitations you will have to work with, depending on the speed of your computer. Another solution is to use special-purpose hardware. Many companies are now manufacturing neural network hardware that can drastically reduce your training time, although, no matter how fast this hardware may be, you will probably find a way to reach that limit also! It is just like closet space: the more you have, the more things you will find to fill it with!

## 1.4 Kohonen self-organizing maps

A Kohonen self-organizing map (SOM) is a neural net consisting of two layers: an input layer and a Kohonen (or output) layer (Caudill, 1993; Hiotis, 1993). These nets can be trained using both supervised and un-supervised learning algorithms. This increases the flexibility of SOMs, which makes them suited to financial prediction.

The output of a SOM is somewhat different from that of the classical neural net. Instead of each of the output neurons providing a result, there is a final step performed between the Kohonen layer and the actual output

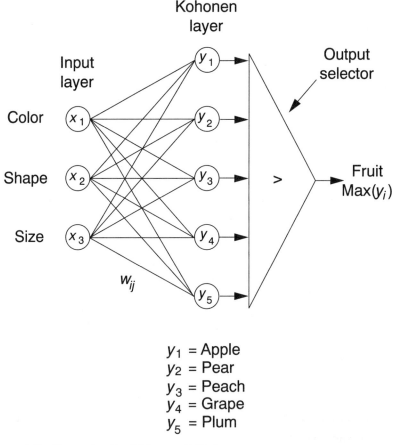

$$y_1 = \text{Apple}$$
$$y_2 = \text{Pear}$$
$$y_3 = \text{Peach}$$
$$y_4 = \text{Grape}$$
$$y_5 = \text{Plum}$$

**Figure 1.7** *Example of a Kohonen SOM.*

of the SOM. This final process simply selects the Kohonen neuron with the highest activation level and declares its neuron number as the output or winner. This architecture makes SOMs make very good classifiers. The number of neurons in the Kohonen layer indicates the number of classes that a SOM will be able to discern. An example of a SOM that classifies fruits based on their characteristics is shown in Figure 1.7.

In this example, three features of fruits are encoded and a maximum of five different classifications will be learned. The activation level of each Kohonen neuron is calculated by Equation 1.8.

$$y_j = \sum_{i=0}^{A} x_i w_{ij} \quad j = 1 \ldots B \qquad (1.8)$$

A simple sum of the weighted inputs is used to generate the output activation levels. The maximum Kohonen neuron is then found and the output is the neuron number that corresponds to a specific category.

The SOM can be trained in either a supervised or unsupervised fashion. The supervised method requires that you know the categories ahead of time, which for many applications is the case. However, if you have an application for which you do not know the final categories, then the unsupervised algorithm is what you need. The unsupervised SOM training algorithm is based upon finding the best match of an input vector to a weight vector of a particular neuron. Once the best match is found, the weight vector is reinforced in the director of the input vector by applying Equation 1.9.

$$w_{ij} = w_{ij} + \eta(x_i - w_{ij}) \qquad (1.9)$$

where $\eta$ is a learning rate that determines how much will be learned from the input vector during each epoch. An unsupervised training algorithm that uses this weight update rule is shown in Figure 1.8.

This algorithm applies each pattern to be classified and determines the winning neuron. The weight vector for the winning neuron is pushed in the direction of the input vector and an error is calculated for each pattern applied. When the total error summed over all patterns during one epoch is less than an acceptable threshold, training can stop. The lower the acceptable error threshold, the more confidence you will have that the SOM has uniquely classified all of the patterns. However, lower thresholds require more epochs to achieve, thereby slowing the learning process. Other techniques for determining when to stop can also be applied. The simplicity of this approach can be deceiving. A SOM can provide surprisingly accurate results when properly applied to a classification problem. Later in the book, I will show you have to use a SOM to classify market conditions into buy, sell and hold recommendations.

The update rule shown in Equation 1.9 is derived from the premise that we are trying to match the input and the weight vectors. The ideal

```
Initialize weights (w ij) to random values
Total_Error = ∞
While Total_Error > Threshold
        Total_Error = 0
        For each Pattern K
                Win = −∞
                For j = 1 to B    /* Find winning neuron
                        y = 0
                        For i = 1 to A
                                y = y + (x i w ij)
                        Next
                        If y > Win
                                Win = y
                                Nwin = i
                        Endif
                Next
                j = Nwin
                Pattern_Error = 0
                For i = 1 to A    /* Reinforce winner
                        e = x i − w ij
                        w ij = w ij + η e
                        Pattern_Error = Pattern_Error + e ²
                Next
                Total_Error = Total_Error+SQRT(Pattern_Error)
        Next
Endwhile
```

**Figure 1.8** *SOM unsupervised training algorithm.*

situation, when the weight vector exactly matches the input vector, is represented by Equation 1.10.

$$w_{\text{new}} - w_{\text{old}} = x - w_{\text{old}} \qquad (1.10)$$

In the very simple case where the number of training patterns equals the number of Kohonen neurons, one epoch with $\eta = 1$ will learn the patterns and is equivalent to simply assigning each weight vector to its associated input vector. In the case of real-life problems, the number of input patterns will normally far exceed the number of Kohonen neurons. For example, in a market timing application, many different market conditions should be classified as a buying opportunity. For this reason, $\eta$ cannot be set to 1, otherwise the learning algorithm will never converge. It will simply oscillate between the various conditions that we want to classify in the same category. The following shows how Equation 1.9 is derived from our desire to have $w$ of the winning neuron as close to $x$ as possible.

Desired for winning neuron:

$$w_{new} = x \tag{1.11}$$

The error of the current winning neuron is:

$$x - w_{old} \tag{1.12}$$

The change from the old to the new weight vector is:

$$w_{new} - w_{old} \tag{1.13}$$

In effect, Equation 1.10 shows that the error between the input vector and the weight vector (Equation 1.12) should be the same as the error between the old and the new weight vector (Equation 1.13). However, we know that this must be a gradual process to avoid oscillation, so we add the learning rate to Equation 1.12 so that only a portion of the error is applied on each iteration and we set the change in the weight vector equal to it:

$$w_{new} - w_{old} = \eta(x - w_{old}) \tag{1.14}$$

Solving for $w_{new}$ we get:

$$w_{new} = w_{old} + \eta(x - w_{old}) \tag{1.15}$$

Equation 1.15 is identical to Equation 1.9 and provides the weight update rule for an unsupervised SOM learning algorithm.

A SOM can also be trained using a supervised learning algorithm. To use this algorithm, one must be able to assign the desired Kohonen neuron number to each pattern before the start of training. Then, the unsupervised algorithm can be used, with some modifications, to convert it to a supervised training algorithm. After the winning neuron of a pattern $k$ is found, a check is performed to determine if the desired winner is the actual winner. If it is, then it is reinforced in the same way as it is in the unsupervised algorithm. If the desired winner does not equal the actual winner, then the desired is reinforced and the actual winner, which has been determined to be incorrect, is penalized by Equation 1.16.

$$w_{new} = w_{old} - \eta(x - w_{old}) \tag{1.16}$$

The supervised training algorithm (Figure 1.9) stops when all of the desired winners equal the actual winners. Knowing when to stop is much easier when using the supervised training algorithm.

A modification can be made to this algorithm to decrease the amount of work that needs to be done during each epoch, thereby speeding up the learning process. The modified algorithm (Figure 1.10) using a verification vector (v) which is equal in size to the number of patterns being classified. Initially, v is set to all false, indicating that each pattern's desired winner is not equal to the actual winner. When a pattern ($k$) generates an output equal to the desired output, v($k$) is set to true. Then, during each epoch, a pattern is not learned when v($k$) is true. When all of v is true,

```
Initialize weights (w ij) to random values
Bad_Map = ∞
While Bad_Map > 0
        Bad_Map = 0
        For each Pattern K
                Win = −∞
                For j = 1 to B    /* Find winning neuron
                        y = 0
                        For i = 1 to A
                                y = y + (x i w ij)
                        Next
                        If y > Win
                                Win = y
                                Nwin = i
                        Endif
                Next
                j = Nwin
                If j = Target
                        For i = 1 to A     /* Reinforce Winner
                                w ij = w ij + η (x i − w ij)
                        Next
                Else
                        Bad_Map = Bad_Map + 1
                        For i = 1 to A     /* Penalize Winner
                                w ij = w ij − η(x i − w ij)
                        Next
                        j = Target
                        For i = 1 to A     /* Reinforce Target
                                w ij = w ij + η (x i − w ij)
                        Next
                Endif
        Next
Endwhile
```

Figure 1.9 *SOM supervised training algorithm.*

v is set back to all false and the process starts again. This is required to ensure that, by learning other patterns, we did not forget patterns we had learned earlier. When a epoch that started with v set to all false ends with v set to all true, the algorithm is completed and all of the patterns have been learned.

```
Initialize weights (w ᵢⱼ) to random values
First_Pass = TRUE
All_True = FALSE
V(1...Npatterns) = FALSE
While NOT All_True
        All_True = TRUE
        Bad_Map = Npatterns
        While Bad_Map > 0
                If NOT V(k)
                        Find winning neuron  (Nwin)
                        If Nwin = Target
                                V(k) = TRUE
                                Bad_Map = Bad_Map – 1
                                Reinforce Winner
                        Else
                                All_True = FALSE
                                Penalize Winner
                                Reinforce Target
                        Endif
                Endif
        Endwhile
        If First_Pass
                First_Pass = FALSE
                All_True = FALSE
        Endif
Endwhile
```

**Figure 1.10** *SOM supervised training algorithm with verification vector.*

## 1.5 Why neural nets are suited for financial prediction

When a person studies the historical data of a particular company, a large number of details must be evaluated in order to arrive at an estimate of the company's future growth potential. Each of the individual pieces of data, such as earnings, stock price, number of shares outstanding and debt position, must be weighed with respect to their importance towards attaining the primary goal: 'TO MAKE A PROFIT!' By examining many different situations when a market advances, we begin to draw various correlations. For example, we may notice that 70% of the companies that have had three years of consecutive earnings growth also have a fourth. So, we think we have found a diamond in the rough. We quickly find five companies that match our criteria and we invest. One year later, with losses on all but one stock, we head back to the drawing board.

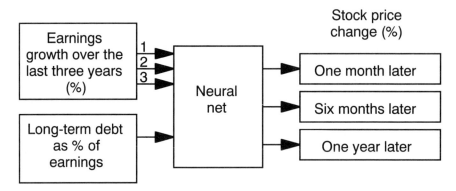

**Figure 1.11** *Neural net architecture for predicting stock prices.*

What went wrong? What did we miss? Eureka! We find out that all of the loosing companies had high long-term debt, so we add another rule to our selection criteria: 'long-term debt < 5% of gross revenues.' The process continues for years and years, until a laundry list of rules for stock picking is established. With a neural net, this whole process can be avoided. A neural net that can learn the best parameters for stock picking can be built. Historical data for numerous stocks can be fed into a neural net, along with known results, and the neural net can learn which parameters indicate that a stock will advance and which indicate that a stock will decline. A block diagram of such a neural net is shown in Figure 1.11.

By selecting a comprehensive sampling of different stocks, at different points within their lifetime, the neural net can learn the expected results for a particular situation. The real beauty of neural nets is their ability to pick up important nuances in the data that we may never think to look for or simply fail to find because of the enormously large search space. A neural net can find these situations so that we can capitalize on them.

The previous discussion centered around using data that is classified as **fundamental** data, and its study is called **fundamental analysis**. (This will be discussed in detail in Chapter 3.) Another branch of market analysis is called **technical analysis**. Technical analysts believe that all of the information one needs to know about a market is contained in its trading statistics, in other words its price and volume data. Who cares what were the fundamental reasons that caused gold to go up, such as fear of impending inflation? The fact is that it went up, therefore the factors that caused it to rise were positive. So how does a technical analyst profit from this? Technical analysts adhere to well-documented chart patterns that have historically demonstrated repeatable results. Neural nets can be used to identify these repeating patterns and predict the future of a market based on them. The characteristic of neural nets that makes them so well suited to this application is that you do not even have to know what patterns you are looking for! The neural net will find them for you by generalizing

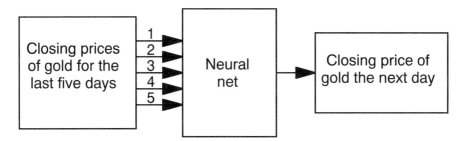

**Figure 1.12** *Neural net architecture for predicting daily gold prices based on a five-day pattern.*

the historical data. A block diagram of how a neural net can accomplish this is depicted in Figure 1.12.

A five-day pattern can be input, followed by the known closing price of the next day. Years of historical data can be learned by the neural net, producing a reliable predictor.

Neural nets can be used to automate certain thinking processes that we must go through in order to predict financial markets. They can classify and generalize enormous amounts of data in complex patterns and in *N*-dimensional space that we cannot begin to visualize. However, there are some obstacles that must be overcome. Neural nets can be overtrained and the financial data we collect does not always lend itself to being processed effectively by a neural net. These are not insurmountable problems. They can be overcome with careful planning and clever techniques that will be presented later in this book.

# 2
# Introduction to the futures markets

If you tell someone you are going to invest in commodities, the next statement will normally be something along the lines of 'Are you crazy!' Many people are afraid of commodities because they simply do not understand them. The commodities markets and their diversity have become quite overwhelming, but once you understand why the markets exist and what they are used for many (but not all) of your fears can be eliminated.

The following introduction to the futures markets is by no means comprehensive. It is intended to give you an overall understanding of the markets and the terminologies surrounding them. This chapter will assist you during the remainder of this book, as these neural net techniques were first applied to the S&P 500 futures contract.

You may have noticed that I sometimes use the terms 'commodities' and 'futures' interchangeably. The broader term, and the one I prefer, is futures. When futures contracts were first established, they were used for actual commodities, such as wheat and corn for example. Later, futures contracts were used for such things as treasury bonds and the stock indexes, which are not commodities in the classic sense of the term.

## 2.1 The futures contract

We will begin our discussion of commodity futures by first defining a **futures contract** and then examining the reasons why the futures markets evolved. A futures contract is an agreement entered into between a buyer and a seller on the floor of an exchange. The buyer agrees to take delivery of the cash commodity and pay the seller the contract price. The seller agrees to deliver the cash commodity, for which he or she will receive the contract price. As we shall see later, both the buyer and the seller may remove the obligation of making and taking delivery of the cash commodity through the process of offsetting their futures positions.

Markets for trading in the cash commodity evolved centuries ago. Buyers and sellers of cash commodities would meet at an agreed location in order to transact business with each other. It was far more convenient for both the buyer and the seller to meet at a specified time at a specified place rather than at diverse locations.

Trading was initially conducted in the cash commodity (spot) for on-the-spot delivery. Trading later evolved in **cash forward transactions**. A cash forward transaction involves an agreement between a buyer and a seller for delivery of a specified amount of the cash commodity to be delivered at a specified time and price at a specified delivery point. For example, the seller would agree to deliver 3500 bushels of wheat to the buyer in 10 weeks at the point specified by the buyer, and the price at the point of delivery would be agreed upon.

In certain respects, the cash forward contract is similar to a futures contract. However, it differs in certain other respects. The cash forward contract could be for any amount of the cash commodity and for any quality, as agreed by the buyer and seller. As we shall see, futures contracts are always for specific amounts of the commodity, for example 5000 bushels of wheat for each contract executed on the Chicago Board of Trade (CBOT), and for a specified grade of the commodity. A futures contract in wheat on the CBOT could never be for any amount other than a multiple of 5000 bushels. The cash forward and the futures contract also differ in another very important respect. The cash forward contract is a non-transferable agreement between the buyer and the seller. Both parties have obligations (the seller to deliver the commodity and the buyer to pay for the commodity on receipt). Usually, neither the initial buyer nor seller could transfer his or her obligation to a third party without the permission of the original partner to the agreement. As we shall see, in a futures contract, both the buyer and the seller may transfer their obligation to a third party without permission.

The futures contract evolved out of the cash forward contract. A futures contract is negotiated on an exchange, which is a central market where all purchase and sale orders are channeled to a single location. A transaction in futures is made on the floor of the exchange between brokers who are members of the exchange. A broker representing the buyer will transact an order with a broker representing the seller. A futures contract occurs when the two brokers transact a purchase and sale.

In summary, a cash forward contract differs from a futures contract in that the futures contract is not personally negotiated between the buyer and seller, it is always for a specified grade and amount of the commodity, and it is delivered from locations and at times specified in exchange rules.

A commodity futures contract is a standardized contract set by a particular exchange and will include the size (5000 bushels, 100 ounces, 42 000 gallons, etc.); the point from which delivery will be made, which is a warehouse or depository approved by the exchange; the grade of the commodity that is to be delivered; and the price of the transaction.

Buyers and sellers of futures contracts both incur obligations. The buyer is obliged to take delivery and make payment for the cash commodity. The seller is obliged to deliver the cash commodity, for which he or she will be paid the contract price. However, both the buyer and the seller have the right to eliminate their obligations through the process of offsetting, which we will examine in detail later.

The grade of the commodity that may be delivered on a futures contract is determined by the exchange on which the commodity is traded.

## 2.2 Long and short positions

The term 'long' is used to describe someone who has an actual cash position. For example, a grain elevator operator who has 1 000 000 bushels of wheat in his or her elevators is long the cash wheat. The term 'short' is used to describe someone who has an obligation to deliver the cash commodity but does not own it. He or she is short cash and will have to buy it at a later date.

Consider an individual who is long 100 000 bushels of wheat that were purchased for $3.00 a bushel and who intends to sell the wheat at some time in the future. From the time of buying the cash wheat until the time of selling it, this individual is vulnerable to a price decline. The price of wheat could drop to, say, $2.90. Selling at this price would result in a loss of $10 000. However, the risk of loss due to a price decline could be substantially reduced by hedging the position by selling futures. If the price of cash declines, the price of futures will usually also decline by approximately the same amount. Let us say that this person sells futures at $3.10 having bought cash at $3.00. When the price of cash declines to $2.90, the price of futures also declines to $3.00. The loss of 10 cents on cash will be matched by a gain of 10 cents in the futures market.

An individual who is not the owner of the cash commodity but is obliged to deliver it at some later date is short cash. For example, a grain exporter agrees to deliver 100 000 bushels of wheat in three months at the current price, which is $3.00 but does not own the cash wheat and is therefore short. Concern that the price of wheat will rise when it is time to buy it to fulfill this commitment can be allayed by buying futures as a temporary substitute for the later cash market purchase. If the price of cash wheat rises, causing a loss, the price of futures will usually also rise. The cash commodity can be bought at the higher price and at the same time the futures can be sold at a higher price. The loss on cash will be matched by a profit on futures.

## 2.3 Speculators

Individuals who trade in futures contracts may be either speculators or hedgers. Speculators buy and sell futures for the purpose of making a profit. Speculators will take a long position (buy futures) when they anticipate that the price will rise. They will take a short position (sell futures) when they anticipate that the price will fall. A speculator who has good judgment will make a profit, but one who makes an incorrect judgment will suffer a loss. Speculators, by entering bids and offers for a commodity, add to the liquidity of the market. Without the active participation of speculators, a market would be thin, meaning that it would lack sufficient liquidity, and price changes would be more volatile. Most of the volume in futures contracts is attributable to speculators; only a very small percentage of the contracts result in delivery of an actual commodity.

## 2.4 Hedgers

Hedgers are not primarily interested in making a profit through the purchase and sale of futures. Hedgers are primarily interested in shifting their risk of loss on the cash commodity due to adverse price change. Hedgers do this by making a futures purchase or sale to serve as a temporary substitute for a cash market transaction that they will make at a later date. Hedgers are business people who produce or use the actual cash commodity, such as farmers or wheat millers. Hedgers use the futures market mainly as a means of shifting risk due to adverse price changes to other people who are willing to assume the risk. The speculator assumes the risk that the hedger is trying to avoid, and this assumption of risk is one of the most important benefits that the speculator provides to the futures market. The elimination of significant price volatility allows a business to plan accurately by stabilizing cash flow. Futures play a critical role in keeping many commodity-dependent businesses running smoothly.

Another business that benefits from the futures markets is mutual funds. A mutual fund manager who sees an impending decline in the stock market can sell a futures contract to hedge the portfolio, rather than selling and buying again. This approach avoids needless commissions and reduces the volatility of the fund.

# 3
# Introduction to technical analysis

All of the prediction techniques presented in this book can be classified as technical analysis. We will be taking historical time series data and using it to predict the future. When I was first presented with this concept I had serious doubts that it could work with a reasonable level of accuracy. With the help of a friend and many hours at the computer running technical analysis software over and over again, I slowly became a believer. I soon learned that technical analysis is a very important tool that could significantly improve my trading. I also quickly learned that the technical indicators and oscillators, and the parameters used to generate them, were overwhelming.

The most important obstacle to the effective use of technical analysis for predicting markets is determining which mix of indicators and oscillators is most suitable for the market you want to trade and which parameters work best in the long term. The truth is that no one knows exactly how to do this. I often felt like I was very close to the solution, but my testing always found situations that made the technical analysis come to a screeching halt.

Then I was introduced to neural networks while attending Rutgers University in pursuit of my Masters degree. I became very excited about the capabilities neural networks had for classifying, generalizing and especially for finding nuances in data. Their ability to uncover hidden relationships in data encouraged me the most. Could neural networks be the key to technical analysis that had been so elusive to me? I bought a copy of *Exploration in Parallel Distributed Processing* (PDP) by McClelland and Rumelhart (1988), which came with neural network software. I took some German mark historical data that I had and let a neural network learn it and the results were very promising. The effort that followed was tremendous, but, like anything else in this world, what is worth having requires hard work and dedication.

It is important that you have a good understanding of technical analysis and its components in order to apply the techniques in this book properly to your specific application. The following provides an overview of technical analysis, but I suggest you get your hands on one of the referenced books and broaden your knowledge.

## 3.1 Technical analysis versus fundamental analysis

Technical analysis (Murphy, 1986) has been around for many years and is sometimes referred to as **charting**. This is because many of these techniques were developed by the painstaking creation of paper and pencil charts representing market activity. Charting is, in many ways, an art. I have seen many individuals use charting tools in a variety of ways, all based on personal preferences and desired goals. Surprisingly, though, good chartists, presented with the same data, will make remarkably similar conclusions, given the same length of time.

What is technical analysis?

Technical analysis is the study of market action, primarily through the use of charts, for the purpose of forecasting future price trends.

The neural network approaches presented in this book can be classified as technical analysis as we are using only the price data to generate the prediction. The alternative to technical analysis is **fundamental analysis**.

Fundamental analysis is the study of the economic forces of supply and demand, for the purpose of forecasting future price trends.

The primary difference between these fields of study is that the fundamentalist studies the *causes* of market movements, while the technician studies their *effects*. We will not be concerned with fundamental analysis in this book, although the use of economic data in the training of a neural network would be an area of further interest.

The concept of fundamental analysis is intuitively logical. The premise is that if one can accurately analyze the supply factors that affect a particular commodity, while simultaneously estimating market demand, one can take advantage of imbalances that ultimately affect the price of the commodity. If you read a news report that finds that drinking coffee has been proven to make you smarter, you can analyze the situation and determine that the demand for coffee is going to increase. If you also discover that supply factors will remain relatively unchanged, you can deduce that the price of coffee will increase. The problem is, how correct are your assumptions and is the timing of the information and the price movement such that you can take advantage of it?

With technical analysis, this problem is eliminated. Technical analysis assumes that, at any instant, all of the forces of supply and demand are factored into the price of a commodity. Imagine that you made your coffee analysis and you call your broker and buy coffee the next morning. Then, one week later, the price of coffee is unchanged. A fundamentalist will assume either that the news did not have the anticipated significance or that some factors were missing from the analysis. In fact, some information will always be missing from the analysis. It is impossible for any one person to know all the detailed factors that may or may not affect a particular market.

In contrast, the technician knows that the only true barometer of a market is price. A technician will look only at how the price (and volume) is reacting to various market situations and, when the equations of the analysis are satisfied, generate a buy or sell. There is obviously much more to technical analysis than this, but that describes it in a nutshell. There is also a kind of nebulous side to technical analysis that contradicts much of its pure chartist nature. Most of technical analysis is quantifiable, but some individuals develop a *feel* for using the indicators that defy the rules. These individuals are few and far between, and if I had been one of them I probably would never have worked with neural networks. As most of us are mere mortals, we must develop a crutch to help us find our way through this difficult process.

## 3.2 Support and resistance

Support and resistance is one of the simplest concepts in technical analysis, yet it is probably the most important of all. First, the basic definition:

Support:    A price level that the market has reached but has not fallen below.

Resistance:    A price level that the market has reached but has not risen above.

When analyzing a market's chart, these level usually stick out like a sore thumb. To find a support level, you simply find an area on the chart, within a selected time frame, where the price could not penetrate and then draw a horizontal line under this level. The opposite can be done to find a resistance level. You will also notice major and minor support and resistance levels. Major levels are prominent on the chart and signify important turning points. Minor levels occur during rallies and declines and are less noticeable. Support and resistance levels are important because prices have a tendency to revisit these levels in the near future. Also, once these levels are broken, two things usually occur: prices will continue in the direction of the breakout and prices will revisit this level on a retracement. When a resistance level is broken, prices will usually continue to rise because a fundamental change has caused prices to increase and because traders who were speculating by shorting the market will cover their positions (buy to accept the loss), which adds fuel to the fire. As you will soon see, a trading system can be developed around these simple concepts. Prices almost never go up in a straight line for very long. Most of the time they will retrace. Retracing is when prices move in the opposite direction to the current trend. Retracements are measured from major support and resistance levels. For example, price level C on Figure 3.1 (1000) represents a 67% retracement of the move from point A (900) to point B (1200). Notice that there is support at 1000 (level C) and resistance at 1200 (level B). However,

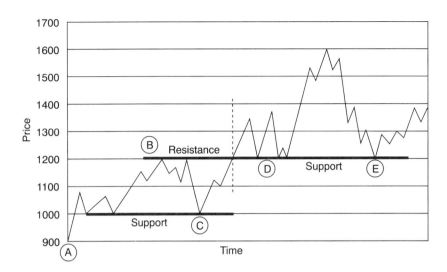

**Figure 3.1** *Support and resistance.*

the 1200 level is broken (dashed line) and then becomes a candidate for a support level. The 1200 level is confirmed as a support level at points D and E.

Resistance becomes support when the resistance level is broken. Conversely, support becomes resistance when the support level is broken.

Another important form of support and resistance is **trend lines**.

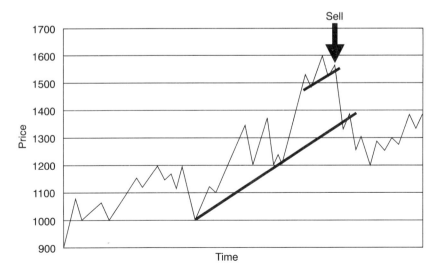

**Figure 3.2** *Using trend lines to detect trend reversals.*

Whereas support and resistance levels are horizontal, trend lines are drawn at an angle. Trend line violations can be used to detect trend reversals, as depicted in Figure 3.2.

## 3.3 Indicators and oscillators

A very useful set of tools used by most market technicians are indicators and oscillators. Indicators and oscillators consist of transformations of price data for the purpose of uncovering hidden features in markets. The primary features we all want to reveal are those immediately preceding a trend change. A common set of indicators and oscillators are classified as **overbought/oversold**. These types of indicators compress price data in a fixed range, usually 0–100. When the indicator nears 0, the market is oversold, and when it nears 100 it is overbought. A market that is oversold will have a tendency to rise and a market that is overbought will have a tendency to decline. A very simple overbought/oversold indicator is given by Equation 3.1.

$$\%K = \frac{C-L}{H-L} \cdot 100 \tag{3.1}$$

where $C$ is the current closing price and $H$ and $L$ are respectively the highest and lowest price in the last $N$ periods. $\%K$ is one component of the stochastic oscillator. Figure 3.3 shows the stochastic oscillator for the S&P 500 futures contract in 1992.

Notice the horizontal lines drawn at the 20/80 levels. These levels are used to interpret the indicator. Full chapters have been written on discussing how to interpret this indicator, but, basically, when the indicator rises above then falls below 80, sell. When it falls below and rises above 20, buy.

## 3.4 Market patterns

Numerous market patterns have been found to exhibit repeatable market moves following their occurrence. These patterns fall into two major categories: **reversal patterns** and **continuation patterns**.

### 3.4.1 Reversal patterns

The five major reversal patterns (Figure 3.4) are:

1. double bottom/top
2. triple bottom/top
3. head and shoulders and inverse head and shoulders

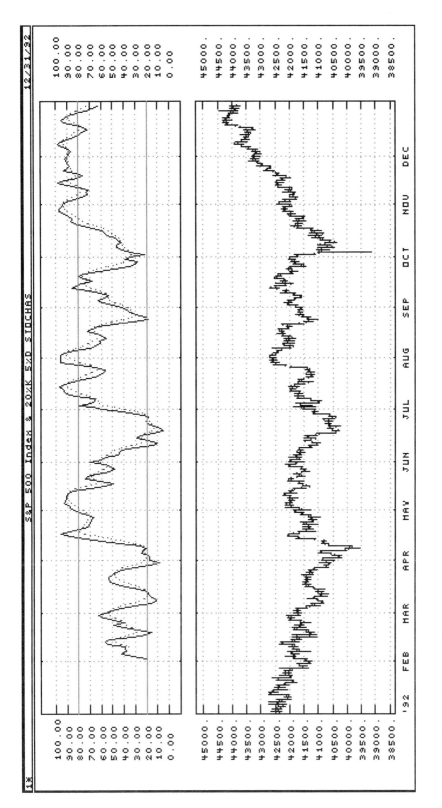

Figure 3.3 *Stochastic oscillator.*

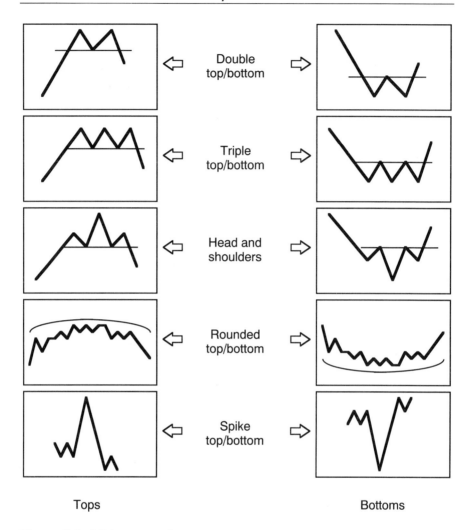

Figure 3.4 *Major reversal patterns.*

4.    rounded bottom/top
5.    V-formations or spikes.

The correct identification of these patterns can be very effective in determining significant trend reversals. Unfortunately, identification of these patterns can be highly subjective and prone to errors. The neural network approaches in this book will, in effect, be recognizing these patterns, plus other inconspicuous features, to be able to outperform most humans. Using a neural network to perform distinct pattern recognition will also be discussed later in this book.

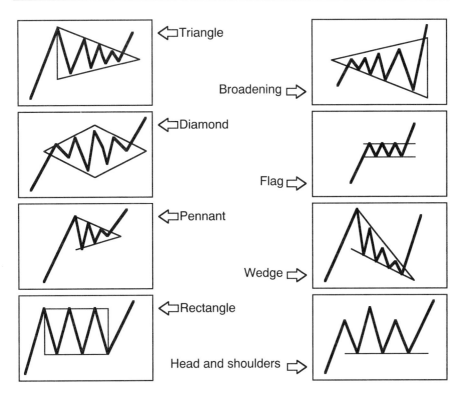

**Figure 3.5** *Major continuation patterns.*

### 3.4.2 Continuation patterns

The major continuation patterns (Figure 3.5) are:

1. triangles
2. broadenings
3. diamonds
4. flags
5. pennants
6. wedges
7. rectangles
8. head and shoulders.

Correct identification of these patterns is very difficult and, in my opinion, is where most technical analysis errors are made. Seeing a pattern in the middle of a chart, two weeks after the subsequent move, is very different from looking at the current data and trying to predict the future. Note also that a head and shoulders can be a reversal pattern or a continuation pattern. Subtle nuances will make all the difference, but even those are not correct all of the time.

## 3.5 Trading systems

A trading system comprises a set of rules for interpreting one or more technical indicators or oscillators for the purpose of making a profit. A trading system provides a rigid framework for making buy and sell decisions by taking the guesswork out of trading markets. A good system will have rules that cover all possible contingencies and which are tightly integrated with a money management scheme. Trading systems are sometimes referred to as **mechanical** systems because of their rigid, disciplined approach.

Most of us, at one time or another, have developed an approach to making money by trading markets. You may see a particular reaction occur to an event or maybe you have picked up on a seasonal tendency. These are probably all good ideas but, unfortunately, most of them are unproven and, worst of all, they are very difficult to test. A mechanical trading system can overcome the testing problem. Because of its definitive nature, historical data can be passed through a mechanical trading system and the results can be compared and contrasted. The neural net approaches presented in this book are ideally suited to being incorporated into a mechanical trading system. The nets' output can be used as the input to a set of rules for determining changes in market trends. Anyone who has traded markets for an extended period of time knows that it can be mentally, emotionally and physically demanding. A mechanical trading system can relieve this stress, or at least minimize it. Most professional money managers use a mechanical system for trading at least a portion of their portfolios (Stein, 1990). Some common examples of mechanical training systems are the moving average system, the breakout system and oscillator-based systems.

### 3.5.1 Moving average system

A simple moving average is defined by the following equation:

$$\text{MA}_i = \frac{1}{N} \left( \sum_{j=0}^{N-1} C_{i-j} \right) \quad i = 1 \dots P \tag{3.2}$$

where $N$ is the length of the moving average and $P$ is the length of the period to average. The result is shown in Figure 3.6. As can be seen, the moving average provides a smoothing of the data. Many systems have been developed based on moving averages. The simplest system has the following rules. When the closing price exceeds the moving average, a buy signal is

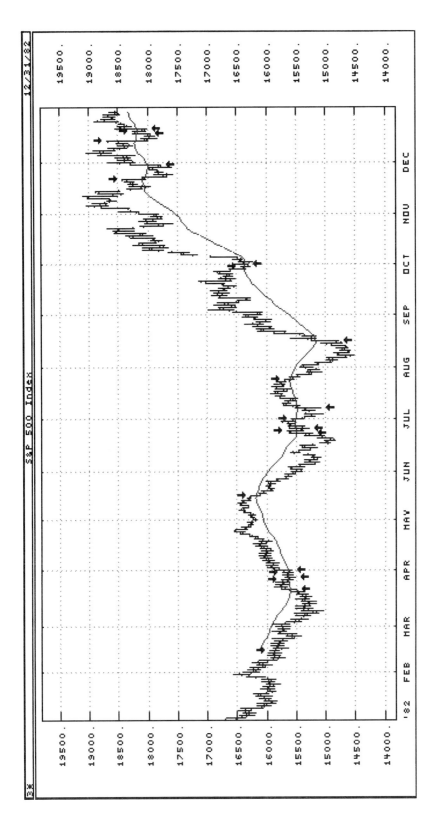

Figure 3.6 *Moving-average system example.*

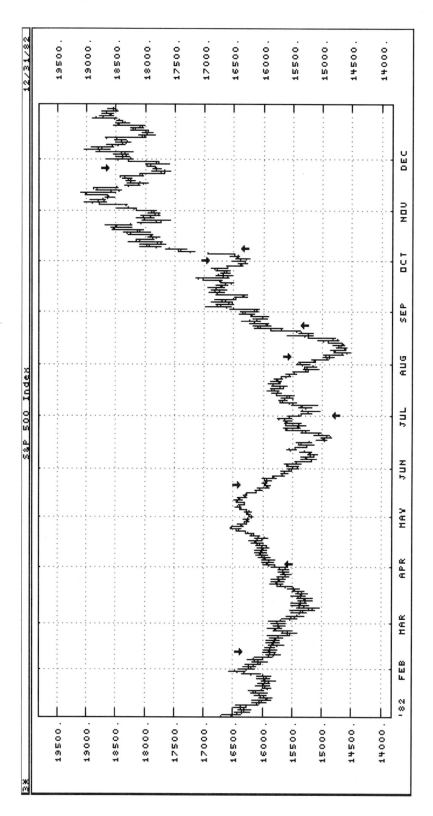

Figure 3.7 *Breakout system example.*

generated, and when the moving average exceeds the closing price, a sell signal is generated. The arrows (up = buy, down = sell) on Figure 3.6 depict the signals from a 20-day moving average ($N = 20$) on the S&P 500 for 1982.

Many variations exist for moving average systems. Some use two moving averages, one slow and one fast, and generate a signal when they cross. An exponentially smoothed moving average can be used, which weights the most recent data higher than older data.

The primary drawback to this type of system is that they are slow, which means that you miss the beginning and end of every move. They also **whip-saw**, which is the problem of repeatedly generating buy and sell signals when the price data goes into a sideways pattern. The advantage of moving average systems is that they are easy to use and understand and they guarantee that you will be in every major price move.

### 3.5.2 Breakout systems

A **breakout system** is one that generates a signal when the price breaks out of a defined range. A simple breakout system is one based on the **four-week rule** as follows:

- Buy when the price exceeds the highest high made in the preceding four weeks.
- Sell when the price falls below the lowest low made in the preceding four weeks.

The S&P 500 signals generated for this system in 1982 are shown in Figure 3.7. This system can be optimized for various markets by adjusting the time period. Instead of using a four-week period, shorter periods can be used. Also, entry and exit rules can be different. For example, a four-week entry rule can be used with a two-week exit rule. The advantage and disadvantages of this system are the same as the moving average system.

### 3.5.3 Oscillator-based systems

Oscillator-based systems use overbought- and oversold-type indicators to generate buy and sell signals. One of the most common indicators of this type is the relative strength index (RSI), developed by J. Welles Wilder Jr. RSI is defined by the following equations:

$$RS = 100 - \frac{100}{1 + RS} \tag{3.3}$$

$$RS = \frac{\text{Average of up closes over the last } N \text{ days}}{\text{Average of down closes over the last } N \text{ days}} \tag{3.4}$$

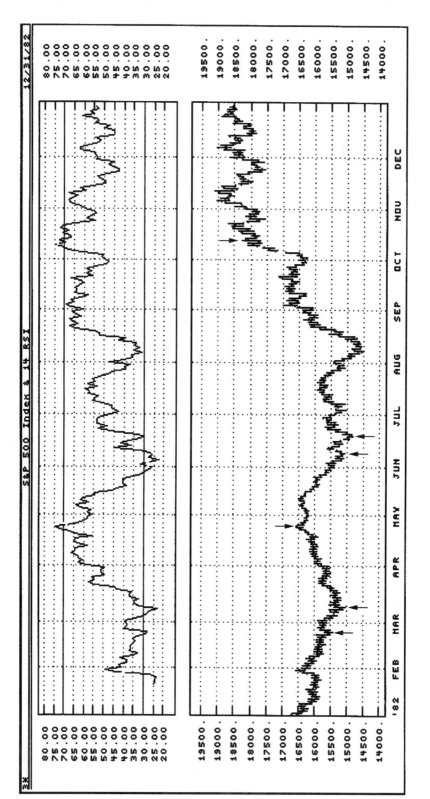

Figure 3.8 *RSI system example.*

An example of a 14-day RSI for the S&P 500 in 1982 is depicted in Figure 3.8. Typical systems of this type define thresholds for determining when to buy and sell. For RSI, 30/70 or 20/80 is normally used. The rules based on a 30/70 RSI system are as follows:

• When RSI falls below 30, then rises above 30, buy.
• When RSI rises above 70, then falls below 70, sell.

Oscillator-based systems work well in a market that fluctuates in a trading range, but do not work as well in a trending market.

# 4
# Survey of neural network literature on financial prediction

The development of an accurate financial predictor is the holy grail of Wall Street. The use of neural networks is just one of the many techniques applied to this task. Within the field of neural networks, there has been an explosion of research, which, in itself, has experienced a great deal of diversity. Various neural net architectures, learning algorithms and testing methods have been researched, but through all this the greatest diversity is in determining which data should be used and how it should be massaged before training. There are many articles in various magazines and papers analyzing the use of neural nets from many different angles, but assembling all of the pieces together into a cohesive system is a difficult, time-consuming task.

In my opinion, neural nets alone will not solve the financial prediction problem. The neural net can provide the core technology, but it must be encased with good feature extraction, signal generation methods and money management in order to provide a complete financial prediction system. This system is actually a **hybrid** system that combines the requisite technologies. The principal reason we do not see the whole picture in the literature is that Wall Street holds its systems close to its chest. It is a very competitive environment and the publishing of a technology breakthrough would only serve to spread the wealth. Consequently, the articles and papers referenced in this chapter provide the pieces of the financial prediction puzzle. The dilemma is determining which pieces to use and in what quantity and combination, in order to build a robust financial predictor.

## 4.1 Research papers

A good starting point is a collection of research papers entitled 'Artificial neural networks forecasting time series' (Rogers and Vemuri, 1990). The papers in this collection cover a wide variety of research and provide a very good set of references for further research. These papers introduce the basic concepts of neural nets, back-propagation and normalizing time series data and also provide in-depth discussions of how they can be applied to real applications. One article in this collection that deserves specific mention is 'Generalization by weight elimination with application to forecasting' (Weigend *et al.*, 1991). An excellent example is presented using currency exchange rates. This paper presents a very important concept called average relative variance (ARV). One of the inherent problems with time series data is that the dynamic range of the data is unknown. The ARV approach converts measurements into relative values, thereby eliminating this problem.

## 4.2 Magazine articles

There is an abundance of articles, in various magazines, that provide overviews of the topic of using neural networks for prediction. A magazine that has published many articles that fall in this class is *Technical Analysis of Stocks and Commodities*. This magazine is targeted at futures traders. The depth of most of the articles in this magazine usually falls short of what is required to develop a complete predictor, but the ideas presented are very timely and innovative. This is because the magazine has a diverse target audience. Articles published by this magazine include 'Neural net input optimizations' (Druey, 1995), 'Beating the market with an expert trading system' (Felsen, 1990), 'A hybrid system for market timing' (Fishman and Barr, 1991), 'Using neural nets in market analysis' (Fishman *et al.*, 1991), 'Archiving the experts' (Glazier, 1990), 'Neural nets in technical analysis' (Lung Shih, 1991), 'The basics of developing a neural trading system' (Mendelsohn, 1991), 'Pattern recognition and candlesticks' (Wagner and Matheny, 1991) and 'The neural network financial wizards' (Ward and Sherald, 1995). These articles provide good overviews of how to use neural nets and artificial intelligence (AI) for market analysis and for developing trading systems. They also provide a good, top-level overview of the advantages and disadvantages of neural network approaches.

Another very good source for neural network literature is *AI Expert* magazine. This magazine has good articles on neural nets and other related AI technologies. From time to time, it publishes articles that can be applied to forecasting and predicting. One such article is 'Understanding conflicting data' (Versaggi, 1995). This article describes some interesting approaches to dealing with neural net patterns that conflict with each other, which can be a problem when dealing with historical price data.

*Futures* magazine is another publication targeted toward futures traders. It has published similar articles to those found in *Technical Analysis of Stocks and Commodities*, such as, 'Neural networks: from the chalkboard to the trading room' (Stein, 1991a), 'The care and feeding of a neural network' (Jurik, 1992) and 'How to build an artificial trader' (Ruggerio, 1994a). These articles are very informative in that they discuss the real-world advantages and disadvantages of using a neural net as the heart of a mechanical trading system.

# Part Two

## Trend Prediction Techniques

# 5
# Basic strategy for trend prediction

This chapter provides all of the basic building blocks necessary to perform trend prediction with a multilayered, feed-forward neural net (Bailey and Thompson, 1990; Fishman *et al.*, 1991; Lowe and Webb, 1991; Mendelsohn, 1991; Tang *et al.*, 1991; Ruggerio, 1994a). The entire process is explained using a test case and a selected technique in each of the various steps of the process. Subsequent chapters will present other improvements and variations on this process.

The following are the five basic processes that must be performed in order to establish a neural net that can predict trends:

- feature extraction
- neural net configuration
- training the net
- signal generation
- walk-forward testing.

Each of these five steps is explained, followed by the results obtained using the example test case.

## 5.1 Feature extraction

Feature extraction is the process whereby the raw input data is transformed into input/target pairs. These patterns represent the entire body of information that we want the net to learn. They must therefore be complete and at the same time be sufficiently general that the net can predict situations that are similar, but not identical, to those used to create the patterns. As humans, we do this all the time. A good example of our generalization capabilities is demonstrated when we read handwriting. No two people, or even the same person, writes a letter the same way each time, yet we can recognize the writing. This is because we have extracted features of the letters as opposed to the specific details. We look at the position of the strokes and where they are connected, not the precise point at which they intersect. The same concept applies to feature extraction of market data. No two market advances look exactly the same, but there are certain characteristics that have repeated themselves over the years: some more than others. We must capture these characteristics in our patterns.

The overriding challenge for feature extraction of market data, such as the S&P 500 index, arises because the upper bound is unknown. Markets will make new highs or plunge to new lows not seen in decades. Our feature extraction technique must deal with this uncertainty and produce robust patterns that accurately represent current and future market conditions. To solve this problem, we will calculate an estimate of the dynamic range and use it in the feature extraction process. In order to train the net we need inputs and targets. The inputs to the net are generated by the formula in Equation 5.1. I will refer to this as the **linear normalization** approach because of the linear manner in which the data is analyzed. Later in the book, other non-linear approaches will be presented. The pattern inputs for each day are calculated as follows:

$$x_j = \frac{c_i - c_{i-j}}{c_i \lambda_j} \quad j = 1 \ldots A, \ -1 \leq x_j \leq 1 \tag{5.1}$$

where $\lambda$ is a vector of precalculated scaling factors (estimates of the dynamic range) given by Equation 5.2.

$$\lambda_j = \frac{2}{P - A} \sum_{i=A+1}^{P} \frac{|c_i - c_{i-j}|}{c_i} \quad j = 1 \ldots A \tag{5.2}$$

The $\lambda$ vector represents what I call the probable volatility window. This approach is based on the concept that, most of the time, the percentage change in closing prices will be in a range of $-\lambda_j$ to $+\lambda$. This provides for a good dynamic range of $x_j$. $\lambda$ is calculated before building the input patterns and $P$ is the number of days being analyzed. This artificial dynamic range is calculated by finding the average percentage change for each of the inputs to the net from $i - 1$ to $i - A$. Two times this average is considered the maximum percentage change that a market will move. Extreme days will occur, at which time the net input value will be clipped at the maximum or minimum value. This is acceptable as extreme days are simply categorized as such by this technique.

The heart of the feature extraction (Equation 5.1) calculates the difference between the current day's closing price ($c_i$) and the previous $A$ closes ($c_{i-j}$). This difference is then normalized by dividing it by the closing price (which results in the percentage change from day $i$ to day $i-j$) and applying the scaling factor $\lambda$ given by Equation 5.2. This value is bounded to the range $-1$ to $+1$, which corresponds to the inputs accepted by the sigmoid activation function. In practice, some values slightly greater than $-1$ and slightly less than $+1$ are used as the sigmoid function does not vary much at its outer limits. I have used $-0.95$ and $+0.95$ in most of my research. Each input to the net becomes a scaled representation of how the current day's close compares with the previous $A$ days. The net will

**Table 5.1** Example price data

| Day $i$ | Closing price, $c_i$ |
|---------|---------------------|
| 1 | 550 |
| 2 | 525 |
| 3 | 500 |
| 4 | 510 |
| 5 | 490 |
| 6 | 490 |
| 7 | 500 |
| 8 | 540 |
| 9 | 580 |
| 10 | 560 |
| 11 | 580 |
| 12 | 600 |

be able to generalize from these inputs to determine when to buy and sell, when coupled with the proper output targets.

Here is a small example of how these formulas transform your raw input data (prices) into neural net inputs. First, we will start with some sample price data for our training period (Table 5.1). The training period length ($P$) is 12, and analysis window size is 4 ($A = 4$). Next, we will need to compute $\lambda$, the probable volatility window. To do this, eight columns have been added to Table 5.1 for $\Delta_j$ = 'change in price' and $\Delta_j/c_i$ = 'percent change' to produce Table 5.2. The percentage change column is summed and divided by $P - A$ to produce the average percentage change for each input. Note that $P - A$ represents the number of actual training patterns that will be generated. This is because the historical data for $A$ days is required to generate the first pattern, which is for day $A + 1$. The average percentage change for each element of the vector is doubled to produce the probable volatility vector. Now we will apply Equation 5.1 to generate the first input pattern, which is for day 5. To demonstrate the calculations, I have extracted the first five rows of the sample data table and added some new columns (Table 5.3). We have now built one input pattern. The complete table of inputs for the example is given by Table 5.4. Now we must associate a target with each input pattern. The target will represent what we want the net to learn when it sees each input pattern.

The output node's target (desired value) is determined by first generating ideal signals, using a percentage change technique shown in Figure 5.1. In other words, when the price advances by more than the $\Delta\%$, the day on which the lowest close was made ($q_{low}$) is flagged as an ideal buy signal ($y = 0.05$). When the price declines more than $\Delta\%$, the day on

**Table 5.2** Probable volatility vector calculations

| $i$ | $c_i$ | $\Delta_1$ | $\Delta_1/c_i$ | $\Delta_2$ | $\Delta_2/c_i$ | $\Delta_3$ | $\Delta_3/c_i$ | $\Delta_4$ | $\Delta_4/c_i$ |
|---|---|---|---|---|---|---|---|---|---|
| 1 | 550 | | | | | | | | |
| 2 | 525 | | | | | | | | |
| 3 | 500 | | | | | | | | |
| 4 | 510 | | | | | | | | |
| 5 | 490 | 20 | 0.041 | 10 | 0.020 | 35 | 0.071 | 60 | 0.122 |
| 6 | 490 | 0 | 0.000 | 20 | 0.041 | 10 | 0.020 | 35 | 0.071 |
| 7 | 500 | 10 | 0.020 | 10 | 0.020 | 10 | 0.020 | 0 | 0.000 |
| 8 | 540 | 40 | 0.074 | 50 | 0.093 | 50 | 0.093 | 30 | 0.056 |
| 9 | 580 | 40 | 0.069 | 80 | 0.138 | 90 | 0.155 | 90 | 0.155 |
| 10 | 560 | 20 | 0.036 | 20 | 0.036 | 60 | 0.107 | 70 | 0.125 |
| 11 | 580 | 20 | 0.034 | 0 | 0.000 | 40 | 0.069 | 80 | 0.138 |
| 12 | 600 | 20 | 0.033 | 40 | 0.067 | 20 | 0.033 | 60 | 0.100 |
| Totals | | | 0.307 | | 0.414 | | 0.569 | | 0.767 |
| Average | | | 0.038 | | 0.052 | | 0.071 | | 0.096 |
| $\lambda_j$ | | | 0.077 | | 0.104 | | 0.142 | | 0.192 |

**Table 5.3** Calculation of first pattern

| Day $i$ | Closing price, $c_i$ | $j$ | $c_i - c_{i-j}$ | $x_j$ |
|---|---|---|---|---|
| 1 | 550 | 4 | −60 | −0.639 |
| 2 | 525 | 3 | −35 | −0.502 |
| 3 | 500 | 2 | −10 | −0.197 |
| 4 | 510 | 1 | −20 | −0.532 |
| 5 | 490 | | | |

**Table 5.4** Complete set of patterns for example price data

| Day $i$ | $x_1$ | $x_2$ | $x_3$ | $x_4$ |
|---|---|---|---|---|
| 5 | −0.532 | −0.197 | −0.502 | −0.639 |
| 6 | 0.000 | −0.394 | −0.143 | −0.373 |
| 7 | 0.261 | 0.193 | −0.141 | 0.000 |
| 8 | 0.950 | 0.894 | 0.651 | 0.290 |
| 9 | 0.899 | 0.950 | 0.950 | 0.809 |
| 10 | −0.465 | 0.345 | 0.753 | 0.652 |
| 11 | 0.449 | 0.000 | 0.485 | 0.719 |
| 12 | 0.434 | 0.644 | 0.234 | 0.522 |

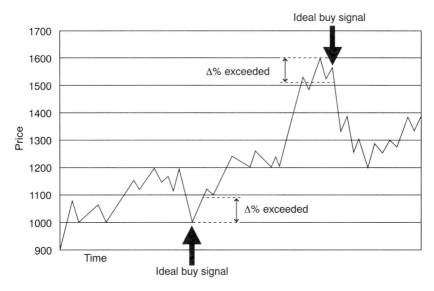

**Figure 5.1** *Percent change technique for generating ideal signals.*

which the highest close was made ($c_{high}$) is flagged as an ideal sell signal ($y = 0.95$). The desired values for days between a buy and a sell signal are normalized based on the closing price as shown in Equation 5.3.

$$d_i = \frac{c_i - c_{low}}{c_{high} - c_{low}} \qquad (5.3)$$

To demonstrate the basic strategy for trend prediction, we will use the S&P 500 futures contract during 1990. Ideal signals using the methods described above are depicted in Figure 5.2* along with the actual S&P 500 futures data used to generate these signals. An excerpt from the pattern file is shown in Table 5.5.

Note that ideal signals look suspiciously like one of the technical oscillators described in Chapter 3. This is no accident. What we have produced with the feature extraction is a **neural net oscillator**. The shape, appearance and use of the neural net oscillator is not unlike that of an RSI. When the neural net oscillator rises above a sell threshold, it signals an alert that the market is approaching a trend change to the down side. When the neural net indicator falls below a buy threshold, it signals an alert that the market is approaching a trend change to the up side.

---

*Note that the ideal signals do not have a specified scale. The vertical placement is set to correspond to the data that was used to generate them and the range is from 0 to 1.

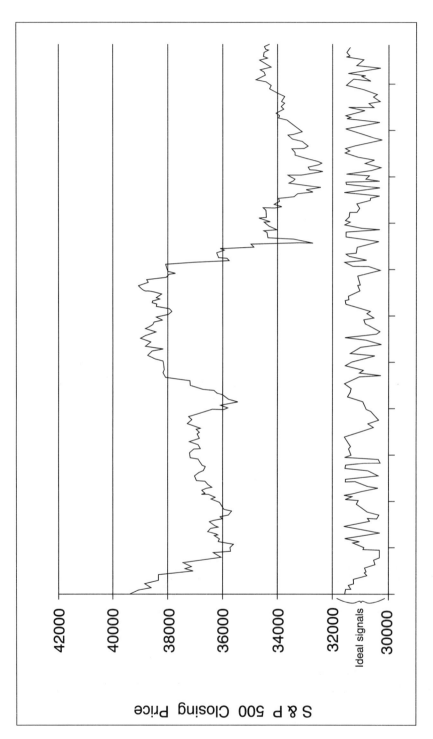

**Figure 5.2** *Ideal signals for 1990.*

Table 5.5 Excerpt from a pattern file (1990)

| Date | $x_1$ | $x_2$ | $x_3$ | $x_4$ | $x_5$ | $x_6$ | $x_7$ | $x_8$ | $x_9$ | $x_{10}$ | $d_1$ |
|---|---|---|---|---|---|---|---|---|---|---|---|
| 19900108 | 0.95 | 0.95 | 0.95 | 0.95 | 0.946 | 0.95 | 0.95 | 0.95 | 0.94 | 0.508 | 0.95 |
| 19900109 | -0.152 | 0.697 | 0.727 | 0.786 | 0.931 | 0.808 | 0.859 | 0.919 | 0.919 | 0.856 | 0.95 |
| 19900110 | -0.354 | -0.347 | 0.373 | 0.467 | 0.549 | 0.716 | 0.62 | 0.693 | 0.765 | 0.774 | 0.929 |
| 19900111 | -0.95 | -0.942 | -0.854 | -0.166 | -0.021 | 0.104 | 0.296 | 0.24 | 0.333 | 0.419 | 0.788 |
| 19900112 | 0.567 | -0.303 | -0.445 | -0.465 | 0.1 | 0.207 | 0.305 | 0.476 | 0.417 | 0.499 | 0.867 |
| 19900115 | -0.95 | -0.32 | -0.832 | -0.905 | -0.874 | -0.323 | -0.19 | -0.071 | 0.114 | 0.072 | 0.724 |
| 19900116 | -0.176 | -0.836 | -0.36 | -0.817 | -0.884 | -0.872 | -0.364 | -0.242 | -0.127 | 0.053 | 0.7 |
| 19900117 | 0.107 | -0.047 | -0.62 | -0.262 | -0.679 | -0.766 | -0.766 | -0.306 | -0.195 | -0.087 | 0.714 |
| 19900118 | -0.95 | -0.95 | -0.95 | -0.95 | -0.95 | -0.95 | -0.95 | -0.95 | -0.95 | -0.894 | 0.422 |
| 19900119 | -0.353 | -0.95 | -0.95 | -0.95 | -0.95 | -0.95 | -0.95 | -0.95 | -0.95 | -0.95 | 0.375 |
| 19900122 | 0.581 | 0.158 | -0.95 | -0.901 | -0.88 | -0.95 | -0.922 | -0.95 | -0.95 | -0.95 | 0.453 |
| 19900123 | -0.677 | -0.062 | -0.248 | -0.95 | -0.95 | -0.95 | -0.95 | -0.95 | -0.95 | -0.95 | 0.363 |
| 19900124 | 0.422 | -0.172 | 0.185 | -0.01 | -0.95 | -0.837 | -0.84 | -0.95 | -0.921 | -0.95 | 0.42 |
| 19900125 | 0.27 | 0.473 | 0.011 | 0.294 | 0.109 | -0.77 | -0.671 | -0.698 | -0.95 | -0.795 | 0.456 |
| 19900126 | -0.95 | -0.95 | -0.845 | -0.95 | -0.7 | -0.785 | -0.95 | -0.95 | -0.95 | -0.95 | 0.166 |
| 19900129 | -0.238 | -0.95 | -0.95 | -0.859 | -0.95 | -0.738 | -0.816 | -0.95 | -0.95 | -0.95 | 0.135 |
| 19900130 | 0.585 | 0.239 | -0.95 | -0.777 | -0.504 | -0.736 | -0.461 | -0.562 | -0.95 | -0.95 | 0.212 |
| 19900131 | -0.95 | -0.5 | -0.542 | -0.95 | -0.95 | -0.95 | -0.95 | -0.906 | -0.95 | -0.95 | 0.05 |
| 19900201 | 0.01 | -0.901 | -0.402 | -0.47 | -0.95 | -0.95 | -0.92 | -0.95 | -0.863 | -0.946 | 0.05 |
| 19900202 | -0.021 | -0.007 | -0.746 | -0.363 | -0.427 | -0.95 | -0.95 | -0.877 | -0.95 | -0.836 | 0.05 |

The process for determining good threshold values is critical to the success of the oscillator. This process will be discussed later.

## 5.2 Neural net configuration

This phase of the process can be quite challenging and it is accomplished in close coordination with the decisions made during the feature extraction phase. It is necessary to design a net that is sufficiently large to absorb the information that we want the net to learn, but small enough so that the time to train can be minimized. To configure a net we must define the following characteristics:

- the number of input neurons;
- the number of output neurons;
- the number of hidden layers;
- the number of neurons in each hidden layer.

These characteristics can be estimated by analyzing the percentage change used to generate the ideal signals in step 1 and the number of patterns to be learned. For our trend prediction application, the following net configuration analysis can be derived from these characteristics. The number of input neurons for our initial approach is simply the average number of days between ideal signals. The higher the number of days, the larger the size of the net. The lower the number of days, the less information the net will have at its disposal to make its decisions. I have found that between 5 and 20 input neurons can predict trend changes when using the linear normalization approach and a 1% change for calculating ideal signals. The important point is that the number selected should match or exceed the average distance between ideal signals. This is obviously a rule-of-thumb and it does not mean that lower or higher values will not work. Using this estimation technique, I have estimated that the number of input neurons ($A$) for this initial approach is 10. This means that we will be using only the data for the past 10 days to predict a trend change. This is a very short period of time, but increasing this number would affect the complexity of the net and increase the training time required.

The number of output neurons for this application is simply 1. The output of this neuron will become our oscillator and will vary between 0.05 and 0.95. An output of 0.05 is assigned to a buy signal and 0.95 is assigned to a sell signal.

Now the hard part, determining the configuration of the hidden layers. The hidden layers are critical to the success or failure of the net. The number of layers determines the complexity of the problem that can be solved by the net. It is rare to use more than two hidden layers; normally one or two layers are used. We will use one layer for the test case. The number of neurons we place in this hidden layer determines the number of interconnections required (weights), which determines the number of unique trend change situations that our net will be able to predict. The number of situations is directly linked to the number of patterns and their correlation to one another. Equation 5.4 shows the relationship between the number of patterns to be learned and the number of weights in the net.

$$\phi(P - A) = (A + 1)B + (B + 1)C \qquad (5.4)$$

The value of $\phi$ represents the percentage of unique patterns that the net will be required to learn. Solving Equation 5.4 for $B$, we obtain the number of hidden neurons required for our application.

$$B = \frac{\phi(P - A) - C}{A + C + 1} \qquad (5.5)$$

For our test case we get the following:

$$B = \frac{\phi(252 - 10) - 1}{10 + 1 + 1} = \phi 20.167 - 0.083 \qquad \text{(Using 5.5)}$$

If $\phi = 0.5$ then $B = 10.167 \approx 10$, that is if we assume that approximately half ($\phi = 0.5$) of the patterns are unique, we arrive at 10 neurons in the hidden layer ($B$=10). There is a substantial amount of literature available on determining the number of hidden neurons and most of it links the number of input patterns to the number of hidden neurons. I have found that, if you know your feature space well enough, you can usually determine this value more accurately than through the use of analytical techniques. This is especially important for the application of predicting time series data, as in many cases the amount of data available to train the net can be significant.

In summary, our neural net configuration will have seven input units ($A = 10$), one hidden layer with 10 units ($B = 10$) and one output unit ($C = 1$), as shown in Figure 5.3. That gives us a total of 21 neurons and two biases. The total number of weights can be calculated as $(A + 1)B + (B + 1)C$. The '+1' is required to account for the biases. For our example we will have $(10 + 1)10 + (10 + 1)1 = 121$ weights. At this point in the process, we have everything we need to train the net. We have a net configuration defined, with a set of training patterns that we want to learn.

## 5.3 Training the net

In order to train the net, we must first divide the available data into three distinct sets (Pardo, 1991; Ruggerio, 1995):

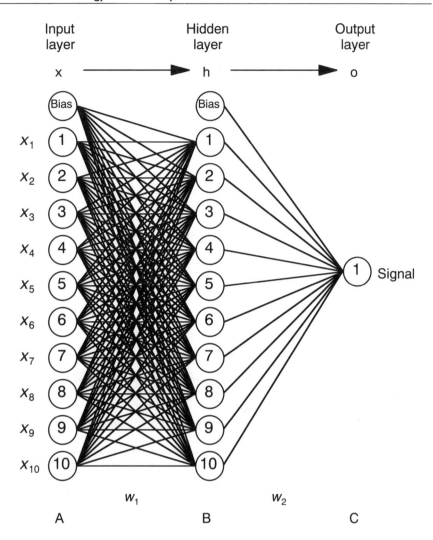

**Figure 5.3** *Neural net configuration for trend prediction test case.*

Set 1: training set
Set 2: parameter set
Set 3: test set.

The training set is used to train the weights of the net, the parameter set is used to determine thresholds for interpreting the neural net oscillator (signal generation) and the test set is used to determine whether or not the trading system is profitable (walk-forward testing). I have always tried to ensure that the sets are in chronological order. For the test case, I have selected three consecutive years, 1990 through 1992, and have made 1990 the training set, 1991 the parameter set and 1992 the test set. This approach is actually arbitrary, but it is natural to process the data sequentially.

The patterns generated in the feature extraction step are used to train the neural net by using the back-propagation learning algorithm. The total sum of the squares (tss) error is calculated after each epoch. Training is determined to be completed when the tss is less than an acceptable error threshold. This threshold is dependent upon the number of patterns that the net is learning and the noise level of the data. The number of patterns is known, but the noisiness of the data is difficult to determine. Conflicts will exist in any normal set of time series data, and these conflicts will determine the noise. A conflict exists when the same input pattern has different targets. If the period of time you select has many of these conflicts, the noise level will be high and, therefore, high tss thresholds will be acceptable. But, if very few conflicts exist, lower thresholds will be desirable. We will normally attempt to achieve an average pss (per pattern) of approximately 0.05. If the test case has 242 patterns to learn, then a tss error threshold of 12.1 may be acceptable.

Another way to determine when to stop training is to analyze the slope of the tss curve over time. With this approach it is necessary stop training periodically and look at the tss curve. If the curve flattens out for a long period of time, then you can assume that the net cannot learn any more. To avoid overtraining, the weights are saved before each break in the training process and the weights saved just after the flattening of the curve are the final weights. This process may be cumbersome, but hindsight is 20/20. The graph shown in Figure 5.4 is the tss error for the training of 1990. Training was stopped after 1000 epochs when the tss curve flattened out at about 27, which was quite far from the target of 12.1. This indicates that there is more noise in our patterns than we anticipated or that the net may not be large enough. One could go back to the feature extraction and net configuration steps at this point and select different parameter combinations. We will continue as this is only a test case.

## 5.4 Signal generation

Signal generation is based on two thresholds which are determined by analyzing the results obtained when passing the parameter data set through the neural net. No additional weight training is performed during this phase. The thresholds to be determined are a minimum (buy) threshold $T_{min}$ and a maximum (sell) threshold $T_{max}$. It is expected that $T_{min}$ will be near 0.05 and $T_{max}$ will be near 0.95. These optimal signal thresholds will be used when determining profits during walk-forward testing.

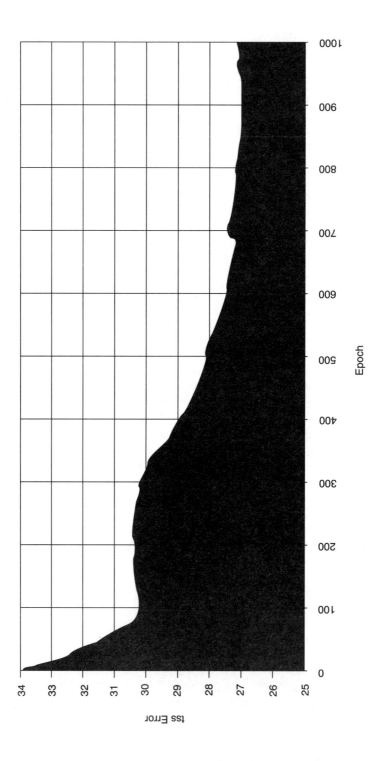

**Figure 5.4** *Graph of tss error for the test case training period (1990).*

Two methods can be used to generate buy and sell signals based on these thresholds:

Method 1   *Buy* when $o \leqslant T_{min}$
           *Sell* when $o \geqslant T_{max}$

Method 2   *Buy* when $o \leqslant T_{min}$ and then $o_t > o_{t-1}$
           *Sell* when $o \geqslant T_{max}$ and then $o_t < o_{t-1}$

Method 1 is identical to the concept used to generate the desired output of the net, that is an overbought/oversold approach. When the net's output ($o$) reaches a predefined threshold, a signal is generated. This method sometimes generates signals too early, causing a great deal of profit potential to be lost. Hence, method 2 was developed. This method only generates signals if $o$ has both reached the threshold and subsequently changes direction. After a threshold is reached, method 2 only requires $o$ to change direction. Method 2 was used to generate signals for the test case. Figure 5.5 contains the neural net output for 1991 when applying the weights learned during the training period. The neural net oscillator was tested using a wide range of combinations for $T_{min}$ and $T_{max}$ and the pair with the best results was selected. $T_{min}$ and $T_{max}$ will be held constant during the next phase, walk-forward testing.

Now we need a method for comparing the results obtained by the various combinations of $T_{min}$ and $T_{max}$. A good measure of how well a neural net can predict trend changes is the profit that can be achieved given an initial investment. But, profit alone does not tell the whole story. The other critical measure of a system's worth is **drawdown**. A drawdown is a period of losses experienced during the test. Drawdown is calculated by subtracting the account value at a peak from the account value at a subsequent low (Figure 5.6). A drawdown is confirmed when the previous peak in profits is exceeded. Until this time, the potential for a greater drawdown exists.

Every loss is in effect a drawdown (derived from the fact that a loss *draws down* the equity in an account). But we will only be concerned with maximum drawdown, or **maxdraw**\*.

The maxdraw is the worst drawdown that a system is expected to experience. Using the profit and the maxdraw, we can establish a good metric for comparing various neural net trading systems. In order to have one number we can use to rank systems, I have developed a relative profit (rprofit%) calculation that uses the maxdraw to adjust the profit (Equation 5.6).

---

\*Many different approaches are used to evaluate trading system's performance (Pardo, 1991; Ruggerio, 1995). For the purpose of this book, maxdraw will be used with profit to establish a metric to evaluate neural net trading systems. These other metrics provide better tools for evaluating a system, but the complex tools required to present them are outside the scope of this book.

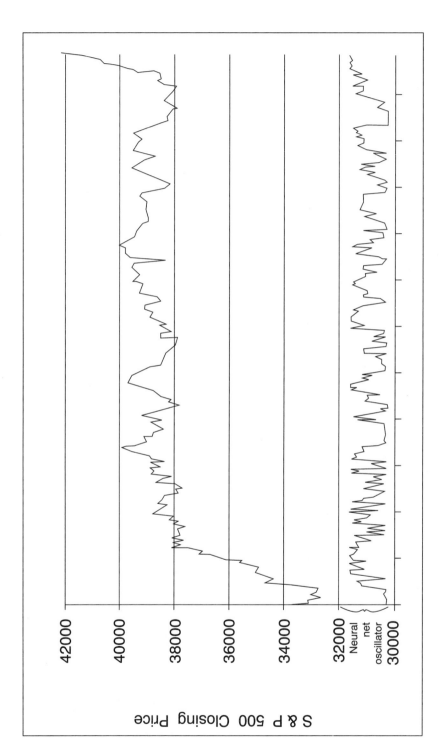

**Figure 5.5** *Neural net oscillator for the parameter set period (1991).*

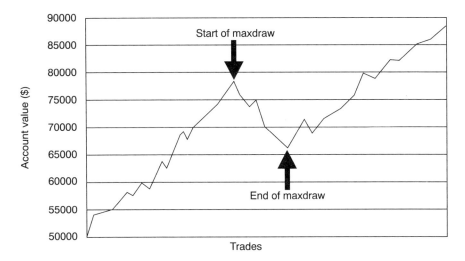

**Figure 5.6** *Drawdown calculation.*

**Table 5.6** Test results from parameter set (1991)

| $T_{min}$ | $T_{max}$ | Profit | Maxdraw | BNAV | Rprofit% |
|---|---|---|---|---|---|
| 0.09 | 0.85 | 4825 | 18 400 | 42 600 | 11.3 |
| 0.09 | 0.86 | 4825 | 18 400 | 42 600 | 11.3 |
| 0.09 | 0.87 | 9325 | 16 800 | 40 200 | 23.2 |
| 0.10 | 0.85 | 4825 | 18 400 | 42 600 | 11.3 |
| 0.10 | 0.86 | 4825 | 18 400 | 42 600 | 11.3 |
| 0.10 | 0.87 | 9325 | 16 800 | 40 200 | 23.2 |
| 0.11 | 0.85 | 4825 | 18 400 | 42 600 | 11.3 |
| 0.11 | 0.86 | 4825 | 18 400 | 42 600 | 11.3 |
| 0.11 | 0.87 | 9325 | 16 800 | 40 200 | 23.2 |
| 0.12 | 0.85 | 4825 | 18 400 | 42 600 | 11.3 |
| 0.12 | 0.86 | 4825 | 18 400 | 42 600 | 11.3 |
| 0.12 | 0.87 | 9325 | 16 800 | 40 200 | 23.2 |
| 0.13 | 0.85 | 4825 | 18 400 | 42 600 | 11.3 |
| 0.13 | 0.86 | 4825 | 18 400 | 42 600 | 11.3 |
| 0.13 | 0.87 | 9325 | 16 800 | 40 200 | 23.2 |
| 0.14 | 0.85 | 4825 | 18 400 | 42 600 | 11.3 |
| 0.14 | 0.86 | 4825 | 18 400 | 42 600 | 11.3 |
| 0.14 | 0.87 | 9325 | 16 800 | 40 200 | 23.2 |
| 0.15 | 0.85 | 4825 | 18 400 | 42 600 | 11.3 |
| 0.15 | 0.86 | 4825 | 18 400 | 42 600 | 11.3 |
| 0.15 | 0.87 | 9325 | 16 800 | 40 200 | 23.2 |

BNAV, beginning net asset value

$$\text{rprofit\%} = \frac{\text{profit} \times 100}{\text{MI} + (1.5 \times \text{maxdraw})} \tag{5.6}$$

where MI is the minimum investment required to trade. This approach scales back the profit achieved for systems with a higher maxdraw. When trading futures contracts, a minimum account value is required to trade. If the maxdraw occurs right from the point we start trading, we want to ensure that we can continue. Also, the maxdraw is obviously not an absolute number, it is only what was experienced through testing. I increase it by 50% in order to provide a cushion for unexpected situations. The denominator of Equation 5.6 actually represents the recommended beginning net asset value (BNAV) to trade the system. For systems that exhibit high volatility, maxdraw will be higher and the starting account value will also be proportionally higher. If system X and system Y both achieve the same profit (in dollars) and system X has a higher maxdraw than system Y, system Y will have a higher rprofit% and will be more desirable.

The rprofit% was calculated for each $T_{min}/T_{max}$ pair, and the one that produced the highest rprofit% was selected. Table 5.6 summarizes the best results obtained for the parameter set in 1991.

## 5.5 Walk-forward testing

The walk-forward approach to testing avoids building a neural net that does not have longevity (Pardo, 1991). Historical data is used to train the neural net and fine tune the signal generation thresholds, then the net is fed data for a period of time it has never seen before. No further fine tuning is performed. This method verifies that the methods used for feature extraction, configuring the neural net, training and signal generation are profitable. If different periods of time are not used for training, parameter selection and testing, you can fall into the trap of developing a neural net that works well only in the time period for which it was developed. Many earlier researchers fell into this trap and gave neural nets a bad name. In recent years, neural nets have gained respect in the financial community.

The results obtained using the parameter set must be analyzed to determine the parameters to be used during walk-forward testing. In analyzing Table 5.5, we can quickly see that a $T_{max}$ of 0.87 produces the most profit and the least drawdown. The $T_{min}$ value can be varied between 0.09 and 0.15 without decreasing the profitability. I selected $T_{min}$ = 0.12, which is the midpoint of the profitable range. The results for the test period (1992) using $T_{min}$ = 0.12 and $T_{max}$ = 0.87 are as follows:

Profit: $6925
Maxdraw: $21 775

$$\text{rprofit\%} = \frac{\$6925 \times 100}{\$15\,000 + (1.5 \times \$21\,775)} = 14.4\% \qquad \text{(Using 5.6)}$$

This shows that an annual 14.4% gain was made on a $48 000 investment. However, a 45.4% drawdown was experienced. This drawdown makes this neural net difficult to trade. The test case demonstrates that the techniques have potential, but further work must be performed in order to reduce the drawdown and make the system more robust. With a few enhancements, this system can achieve at least a 20% annual return, with a smaller drawdown.

# 6
# A mechanical neural net position trading system

The term **mechanical** is used to describe a trading system that has all of the human decision process eliminated (Murphy, 1986; Mendelsohn, 1991; Ruggerio, 1994a). A mechanical trading system must account for every detail, especially those that can adversely affect the bottom line. The first process that must be defined is signal generation, when to buy and sell. Although I will not diminish the importance of signal generation, you will soon see that many other factors are just as important and many beginners leave them unattended. Experienced traders will use a mechanical system as a frame of reference. If factors not used in the development of the system confirm or deny the signals generated by the system, an experienced trader will use this information to augment the trades. The temptation to think you know better than the system must be avoided. Mechanical systems will have drawdowns and you must suffer through these periods. It is common to override the signals during a losing period when you see potential profits left on the table. As long as your actual drawdown has not significantly exceeded the drawdown experienced during testing, you must stick with the system.

In order to round out the basic techniques given in Chapter 5, certain other real-world factors must be considered. The factors can be grouped into the following major categories:

- trading signals
- money management
- risk management.

## 6.1 Trading signals

The generation of accurate trading signals is the heart of any system. Bad trading signals will not be overcome by any of the other factors, but good trading signals can be harmed by improper selection of the other factors. The trading machine must be fine tuned like a car's engine. The spark, the fuel mixture and the piston must all be operating correctly before the engine can operate correctly. Similarly, the trading signals are only one component of the trading machine.

The neural net techniques presented in this book can be used as independent trading signals or they can be combined with other techniques. The combination process is called **filtering**. The primary motivation behind filtering is the removal of losing trades without removing winning trades. A filtering technique using a neural network is presented in Section 8.2.

Signals can be tailored to any relative period of time. Traders generally group them into position trading signals (which generate signals on an end-of-day basis) and day trading signals (which generate signals during the trading day). Position trading time horizons can vary greatly from trader to trader. Some traders feel that a position is old when they have held it for two or three days, while others will hold a trade for 2–3 months. You must pick a trading frequency that is compatible with your personality and the system you have developed. In Chapter 5, I presented a technique whereby a percentage change was used to detect a trend change. High percentage changes will generate less frequent signals, while lower percentage changes will generate more frequent signals. After you have generated a set of signals, examine the data along with the signals and try to envision yourself carrying out the trades, then adjust the frequency so that it fits your trading style. Of course, the market you are trading must also fit this frequency. Some markets will only work using certain periods and your profits may suffer when incompatible trading frequencies are used. You must find an acceptable balance.

## 6.2 Money management

Money management is the process by which you determine how much capital to commit on each trade. It can be based on a simple constant factor, a set progression or other signals generated by your system. In Chapter 5, we used a simple constant factor. Each time a signal was generated, one futures contract was traded. This method is good for verifying the accuracy of a system, but it may not be the best way to commit your money.

To provide an example of how your money management approach can significantly affect the final result, consider the following trading results in Table 6.1

If you traded one contract on each trade, you would be no richer or poorer, as the total sum of the profit (loss) column would be zero. A progressive money management scheme is based on increasing the number of contracts traded as you accumulate winning trades. Table 6.2 provides the results of this approach.

Another approach is to use a regressive scheme based on an expected profit/loss ratio. If you expect two wins for every loss, then the following win regression could be used: 2–2–1–2–2–3–4. It is a good idea never to increase the number of contracts so that you could lose the gains from the previous two trades. Every time you have a winning trade, you advance

**Table 6.1** Money management example trading results

| Trade | Profit (loss) |
|-------|---------------|
| 1 | (300) |
| 2 | 900 |
| 3 | 200 |
| 4 | (500) |
| 5 | (100) |
| 6 | 300 |
| 7 | 400 |
| 8 | (500) |
| 9 | 200 |
| 10 | (600) |

**Table 6.2** Progressive money management example

| Trade | Profit (loss) | Number of contracts | Profit (loss) |
|-------|---------------|---------------------|---------------|
| 1 | −300 | 1 | (300) |
| 2 | 900 | 1 | 900 |
| 3 | 200 | 2 | 400 |
| 4 | −500 | 3 | (1500) |
| 5 | −100 | 1 | (100) |
| 6 | 300 | 1 | 300 |
| 7 | 400 | 2 | 800 |
| 8 | −500 | 3 | (1500) |
| 9 | 200 | 1 | 200 |
| 10 | −600 | 2 | (1200) |
| Total profit (loss) | | | (2000) |

**Table 6.3** Regressive money management example

| Trade | Profit (loss) | Number of contracts | Profit (loss) |
|-------|---------------|---------------------|---------------|
| 1 | −300 | 2 | (600) |
| 2 | 900 | 2 | 1800 |
| 3 | 200 | 2 | 400 |
| 4 | −500 | 1 | (500) |
| 5 | −100 | 2 | (200) |
| 6 | 300 | 2 | 600 |
| 7 | 400 | 2 | 800 |
| 8 | −500 | 1 | (500) |
| 9 | 200 | 2 | 400 |
| 10 | −600 | 2 | (1200) |
| Total profit (loss) | | | +1000 |

to the next number in the sequence. Table 6.3 contains the results when using a regressive money management approach.

As you can see, the same sequence of trades broke even, lost $2000 and made $1000, simply by changing the money management approach.

## 6.3 Risk management

Risk management is another important component of any mechanical trading system. Risk management should actually be called risk minimization. The concept is to reduce your risk as much as possible on each trade. You cannot eliminate risk entirely since there are no sure things when trading markets. Each trade will have risk, but you must determine the amount of risk you are willing to accept and design the size of your trades around that risk.

The most common approach for limiting risk is the use of stop-loss orders or stop orders. By placing a stop order at the same time you enter a market, you have reduced your overall risk to an acceptable level. For example, if you buy one S&P 500 futures contract at $450.00 and you place a sell stop order at $448.00, you have limited your risk to approximately $1000 ($500 per point × 2 points). Note that I said 'approximately.' That is because, when the stop price is reached, a market order is actually placed. The fill price of that market order will determine the actual loss. You could place a stop-limit order, which uses a limit order when the stop price is hit, but this is risky because in a fast market the limit price may never get filled. The stop-market order ensures an exit from the market.

Another problem that exists with stop orders is opening gaps. It is possible that when a market opens it does so at a price below your sell stop (or above your buy stop). When this occurs the market order is triggered and the loss can be much greater than you anticipated. There is nothing you can do to prevent this from occurring. If you cancel your stop you may be taking an even greater risk.

Once you have made your decision to use stops to limit your risk, you must decide where the stops will be placed. There are countless techniques for stop placement. A few of the most common techniques are discussed as follows:

*Fixed stop*
This technique picks a fixed amount to be risked on each trade and places the stop so that the fixed amount is the maximum loss. This technique is easy to implement, but it is not in tune with the volatility of the market.

*Moving average stop*
This technique places the stop at a particular moving average. The advantage of this approach is that your stop moves in the direction

of the market, which can work to protect profits when a trade moves in your direction. The moving average can also be bounded by a fixed amount to ensure that a maximum loss per trade can be maintained.

*Support/resistance stop*
When support or resistance can be found in a market, stops can be placed just below support or just above resistance. This technique works because markets tend to continue in the direction they are headed when a support or resistance level is violated.

The next decision you must make is how much to risk on each trade. The most common approach is to set a limit in terms of percentage of capital that will be put at risk for each trade. The percentage depends upon your risk tolerance and your account size. For small accounts of around $20 000, you will be forced to risk 5–10% of your capital on each trade. This is a very high number for most money managers. Usually, 1–3% is an acceptable amount. To provide an example of how all this fits together, let us make the following assumptions:

- $1000 fixed stops
- $200 000 starting capital
- a regressive money management scheme (2–2–1–2–3–4–5)
- 10% maximum drawdown ($20 000).

Using these assumptions, we have devised a money management system that will risk approximately 1% of the starting capital per trade.

$$1\% = \frac{\$1000 \times 2 \text{ contracts}}{\$200\,000} \tag{6.1}$$

If the maximum drawdown occurs right from the start of trading (seven consecutive losses of $2000, $2000, $1000, $2000, $3000, $4000 and $5000), you would be risking a maximum of 1.1% of your remaining capital on the next, and possibly last, trade.

$$1.1\% = \frac{\$1000 \times 2 \text{ contracts}}{\$181\,000} \tag{6.2}$$

By careful planning and analysis of the risks, you can develop a robust money management system that will significantly enhance your mechanical trading system and eliminate the guesswork.

# 7
# Advanced feature extraction techniques for trend prediction

The techniques described in the previous chapters can be viewed as a starting point for a myriad of different ways in which the feature extraction process can be performed. In this chapter, some variations that have been found to enhance the performance of the net in some circumstances are presented. The best way to measure the effect of these feature extraction enhancements is to compare results on the markets you are analyzing. This can be a very time-consuming process, but, with the use of some common sense and experience with the process, you will be able to shorten the time it takes to determine the best feature extraction technique for your application.

## 7.1 Exponential averaging

In the examples presented so far, we have focused on predicting trend changes using the previous $N$ days in a linear fashion. These techniques work, but they can be improved by incorporating more data so that the net will have an indication of the long-term trend, along with the most recent events. The same pattern over the last $N$ days may result in a different signal depending upon the prevailing trend. If the last three days all posted gains, tomorrow's prediction would probably be different depending on whether the market was in a two-month up trend or a two-month down trend. Most market analysts will agree that the longer term trend has a significant impact on short-term predictions. Therefore, by limiting the window of data that our neural net sees to 10 or 20 days, we are limiting its ability to predict a trend change. The obvious solution is to increase the window size to include enough data so that the longer term trend can be used in our prediction. Exponential averaging is a technique for accomplishing this (Jurik, 1992). For example, we will assume that six months is long enough to have a good indication of the prevailing trend. That means we will need about 132 inputs to our net (six times approximately 22 trading days per month). A neural net of this size is impractical. As the size of the net increases, the time required to train the net quickly becomes unacceptable. The final decision depends upon the processing power to which you have access, but sooner or later it will be a problem.

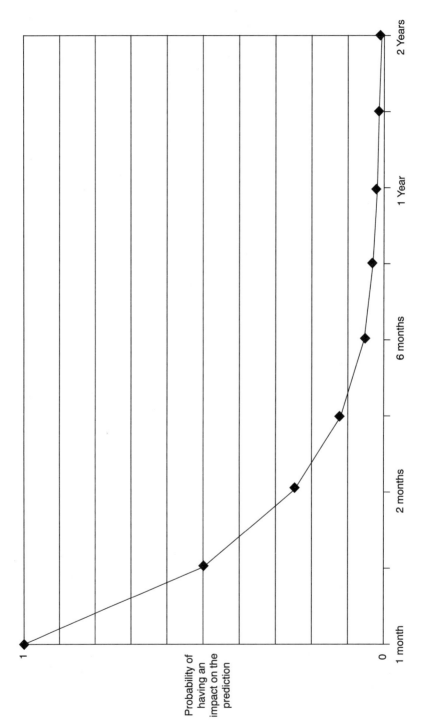

**Figure 7.1** *Probability of impacting prediction.*

Also, many of the inputs will have little or no impact on the prediction so we will end up wasting time and computing resources.

Let us look at the problem from a different angle. Which of the following net inputs have the highest probability of impacting tomorrow's prediction?

> Input 1: $c_i - c_{i-1}$
> Input 2: $c_i - c_{i-20}$
> Input 3: $c_i - c_{i-100}$

Logically, input 1 will be the freshest in every trader's mind and will therefore have the greatest probability of affecting the market on the following day. Conversely, the closing price 100 days ago probably has no impact on tomorrow. Given this to be true, the neural net will learn to ignore this data and it will not improve the performance of our system. We would only succeed in overloading the net with useless information. The important feature is the trend. The importance of the trend diminishes as the trend period increases (Figure 7.1).

The solution to this dilemma is to average blocks of data and present the average to the net. The size of the block becomes increasingly larger, based on an exponential series, as the trend period length increases. The actual size of the block to be used is determined by Equation 7.1:

$$\text{For } j = 1: f_{\text{EXP}}(i, j) = c_{i-1}$$

$$\text{For } j > 1: f_{\text{EXP}}(i, j) = 2^{-j+2} \sum_{k=2^{i-k}+1}^{2^{i-k}} c_{i-k} \tag{7.1}$$

By replacing $c_{i-j}$ with $f_{\text{EXP}}(i, j)$ using Equation 5.1 we get a new feature extraction equation that includes the exponential technique.

$$x_j = \frac{c_i - f_{\text{EXP}}(i, j)}{c_i \lambda_j} \quad j = 1 \ldots A, \ -1 \leq x_j \leq 1 \tag{7.2}$$

This technique expands the window size that is used to present each day's pattern to the net and at the same time minimizes the amount of data that must be used (Figure 7.2). Table 7.1 demonstrates that, by using only 10 inputs, we can have our neural net look at almost two years' worth of data (512 trading days).

Input neurons 1 and 2 will receive the same input as used in the linear technique, but all subsequent input neurons will receive an average of the prices in an ever-increasing block size. The exponential averaging technique is good when the recent historical prices have little impact on the prediction, but for cases where more detail is required the Fibonacci averaging technique may be more suitable.

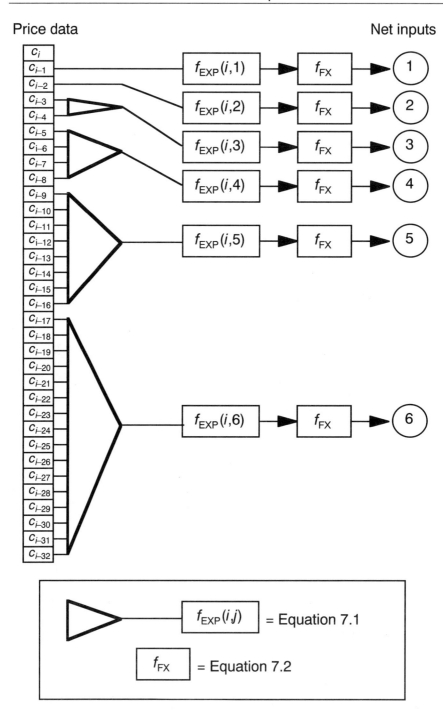

**Figure 7.2** *Exponential averaging.*

Table 7.1 Exponential averaging range compression

| Input neuron | Start pointer | End pointer |
|---|---|---|
| 1 | 1 | 1 |
| 2 | 2 | 2 |
| 3 | 3 | 4 |
| 4 | 5 | 8 |
| 5 | 9 | 16 |
| 6 | 17 | 32 |
| 7 | 33 | 64 |
| 8 | 65 | 128 |
| 9 | 129 | 256 |
| 10 | 257 | 512 |

## 7.2 Fibonacci averaging

Another technique that can be used to expand the amount of data presented to the net is based on the Fibonacci series. This technique is very similar to the exponential averaging technique except that the block size is determined by using the Fibonacci series (Figure 7.3). The Fibonacci numbers are defined as $f(0) = 0$, $f(1) = 1$, $f(i) = f(i-1)+f(i-2)$ for $i = 2 \ldots N$. For $N = 7$, $f = \{0, 1, 1, 2, 3, 5, 8, 13\}$. The Fibonacci series does not accelerate as rapidly as the exponential series and therefore increases the sensitivity of the inputs. This increase in sensitivity is paid for with neurons. The Fibonacci technique can only cover three months of data with 10 neurons (Table 7.2) as opposed to the almost two-year coverage gained by the exponential approach. The advantages and disadvantages must be evaluated for your application through rigorous testing. Between the linear, exponential and Fibonacci techniques, you should be able to find an optimum strategy. You can also create your own series that may be fine tuned to known periods that exist within your data.

## 7.3 Using logarithms

Logarithms can be used during feature extraction to emphasize certain ranges of input or desired output values in order to increase their importance in the learning algorithm and improve the prediction results. The logarithm can be used to compress the input values and place more emphasis on values that may have a greater impact on the learning algorithm. For example, look at the graph in Figure 7.4.

In this example you can see that the change in $x$ is constant (100), but the change in $\log_{10}(x)$ decreases as $x$ increases. Therefore, for our applica-

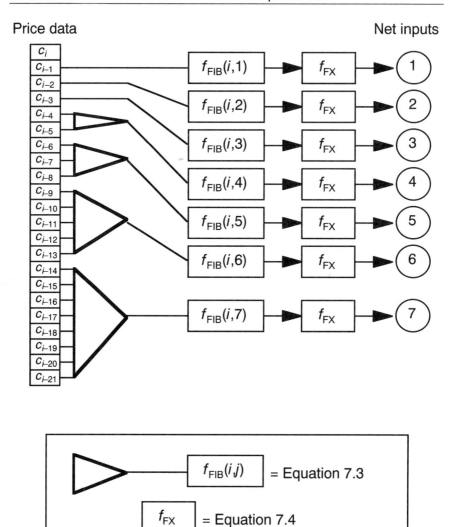

**Figure** 7.3 *Fibonacci averaging.*

tion, the log function will have the effect of masking wild price swings and grouping them into a range that the net can learn. At the same time, the data that falls in the lower ranges will be preserved and will enhance our prediction capability.

We can modify Equations 5.1 and 5.2 to apply this technique as follows:

$$x_j = \frac{\log (c_i - c_{i-j})}{c_i \lambda_j} \quad j = 1 \ldots A, \ -1 \leqslant x_j \leqslant 1 \tag{7.3}$$

**Table** 7.2 Fibonacci averaging range compression

| Input neuron | Start pointer | End pointer |
|:---:|:---:|:---:|
| 1 | 1 | 1 |
| 2 | 2 | 2 |
| 3 | 3 | 3 |
| 4 | 4 | 5 |
| 5 | 6 | 8 |
| 6 | 9 | 13 |
| 7 | 14 | 21 |
| 8 | 22 | 34 |
| 9 | 35 | 55 |
| 10 | 56 | 89 |

$$\lambda_j = \frac{2}{P - A} \sum_{i=A+1}^{P} \frac{\log(c_i - c_{i-j})}{c_i} \quad j = 1 \ldots A$$

$$(7.4)$$

The log's base is not important as we end up normalizing the result into the range acceptable by the neural net ($-0.95 \leqslant x \leqslant 95$). A change in the base will only result in a proportional change in values of $\lambda_j$. The shape of the log function is what is important.

Logarithms can also be used by taking the log of the ratio of closing prices. Up to this point, all of the patterns presented were based on the change in price. Equation 7.5 depicts a new approach to feature extraction.

$$x_j = \log_b\left(\frac{c_i}{c_{i-j}}\right) \quad j = 1 \ldots A, \ -1 \leqslant x_j \leqslant 1$$

$$(7.5)$$

It may seem odd that the $c_i$ term (the reference closing price) is in the numerator as opposed to the denominator, but this approach is preferred as positive inputs will now denote a rise in price and negative inputs will denote a decrease in price. This makes the handling and analysis of pattern data easier. The critical component of this approach is the base ($b$), which is the complete opposite of the previous approach. The base serves to normalize the inputs into the acceptable range ($-1$ to $+1$) as shown in the example in Figure 7.5.

The base performs the same function as $\lambda$ in the previous normalization examples. The base can be determined by using the same method as used for $\lambda$, or it can be set to a known maximum ratio. For example, most market indexes, such as the Dow Jones Industrial Average, seldom

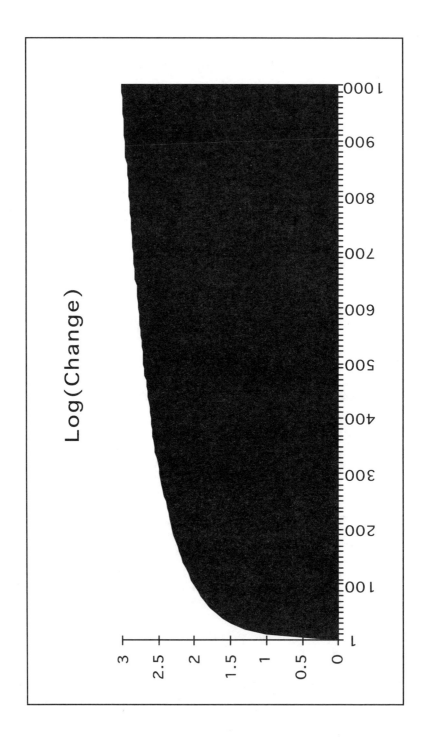

**Figure 7.4** *Logarithm example.*

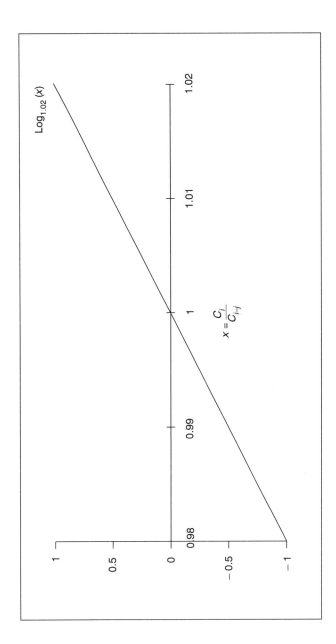

**Figure 7.5** *Logarithm input normalization.*

fluctuate by more than 1% from one day to the next. Based on this fact, we could select a maximum fluctuation of 2%. A 2% maximum fluctuation equates to a base of 1 plus 2% or 1.02. Values that fall outside the acceptable range should be truncated. Care must be taken to ensure that only a few of the patterns use truncated values and that these are truly due to abnormal price movements.

## 7.4 Pattern recognition

All of the techniques presented so far are actually variations of pattern recognition, using automated pattern generation. Pattern recognition as discussed here is based on hand-picking and classifying known, high-probability patterns, and establishing a neural net to recognize them (Lippmann, 1989; Wagner and Matheny, 1991). Two basic approaches will be discussed: distributed and integrated. The terms distributed and integrated are used to describe whether one (integrated) or multiple (distributed) neural nets are used to learn the patterns.

### 7.4.1 Distributed pattern recognition

The distributed approach is based on establishing a separate neural net for each pattern you want to detect. Then a selection algorithm is used to determine if a pattern is recognized (Figure 7.6).

The steps for building a distributed pattern recognition neural net are as follows:

Step 1: Locate the point in the data where each pattern is completed.
Step 2: Build a pattern record for each of the points identified in step 1. Assign it to a pattern code from 1 to the number of patterns.
Step 3: Duplicate the pattern file for each neural net and assign a desired output of 1 to each pattern record associated with the net and zero to all the others.
Step 4: Train each neural net using the pattern records built specifically for it.
Step 5: Develop a selection algorithm.

*Step 1*

Before you can begin developing a pattern recognition neural net, you must determine which patterns you want to recognize and which patterns you do not want to recognize. The market patterns used by technical analysts were presented in Figures 3.4 and 3.5. The major reversal patterns (Figure 3.4) are a good place to start as these patterns represent where we would like to buy or sell a market. The continuation patterns (Figure 3.5) are also very important. Without these, the neural net will not have a

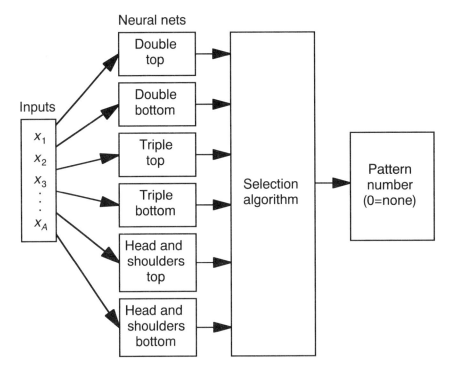

**Figure** 7.6 *Distributed pattern recognition.*

frame of reference. The process of picking the day a pattern has completed and the method used for determining the number of input neurons are closely related. You must pick a day far enough toward the end of the pattern so that it is not confused with other similar patterns and, at the same time, you should try to minimize the width of the pattern (which equates to the number of neurons). If the pattern is too wide, the recognition will be too late to be profitable. The key to success lies in the neural net's ability to pick up on variations in the patterns and to distinguish them in noisy environments, so your pattern generation process should be tailored to reach this goal.

One way to reduce the input data and maintain the pattern's shape is to compress similar directional movements into a single input. This will preserve the shape, which is what we need to recognize, and simplify the net as a fixed number of inputs will always represent a pattern. An example of this technique, called shape extraction, is shown in Figure 7.7.

Depending upon your time horizon, you may want to include a threshold for determining when to change direction. This is especially true if you are attempting to detect patterns much longer in time than the frequency of your data.

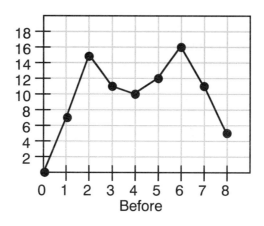

Before

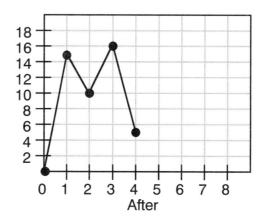

After

| Day | Before | After |
|-----|--------|-------|
| 1 | +7 | |
| 2 | +8 | +15 |
| 3 | −4 | |
| 4 | −1 | −5 |
| 5 | +2 | |
| 6 | +4 | +6 |
| 7 | −5 | |
| 8 | −6 | −11 |

2:1 Compression

**Figure** 7.7 *Shape extraction.*

*Step 2*

When using the distributed pattern recognition approach, the same pattern file is presented to each neural net, except that each pattern will have different target values. This step is used to assign a unique value to each similar pattern. Using the six patterns identified in Figure 7.6, we can make the following arbitrary assignments:

Pattern 1: double top
Pattern 2: double bottom
Pattern 3: triple top
Pattern 4: triple bottom
Pattern 5: head and shoulders top
Pattern 6: head and shoulders bottom.

*Step 3*

Now we must create a unique pattern file for each neural net, 1 through 6. The targets depend upon the neural net it is being used to train. For example, if we are establishing the double top pattern file, then all of the patterns that identify a double top (pattern 1) will have a target value of 1 and all of the other patterns will have a target value of 0. The following algorithm can be used:

```
for patno = 1 to no_of_patterns
        open pattern file patno
        for each pattern in the file
                if patno = target_value
                        target_value = 1
                else
                        target_value = 0
                endif
        endfor
        close file
    endfor
```

*Step 4*

Each neural net must now be trained using its specific pattern file. The neural net will learn to output a 1 only when it sees the pattern it has been designated to recognize. All of the other patterns will cause the net to output a 0 when they are detected. If new patterns are encountered that the neural net was not trained on, it will probably output a value between 0 and 1. The selection algorithm will be responsible for determining how to deal with this uncertainty.

*Step 5*

This is a critical step as it is used to make our final determination as to whether or not a given pattern has been identified. Unfortunately, the patterns that will exist in the future do not exactly match the ones we have used to train our neural nets. Therefore, each neural net will output not only ones and zeros, but any value in that range. The selection algorithm must determine how to interpret these outputs and make the correct identification. A good approach to designing this algorithm can be found in a method called output thresholding. Output thresholding is based on three parameters, $t_1$, $t_2$ and $t_d$ defined as follows:

$t_1$: the minimum output level of the most active output unit required to be considered recognized

$t_2$: the maximum output level of the second most active output unit.

$t_d$: the minimum distance between the activity level of the most active output unit and the second most active output unit.

Given these three parameters, the following conditions must be true for a pattern to be positively identified:

Condition 1: The neural net's output unit must be greater than $t_1$.

Condition 2: The output units of all of the other neural nets must be less than $t_2$.

Condition 3: The difference between the highest neural net output unit and the second highest neural net output unit must be greater than $t_d$.

The exact values for the three parameters will vary based on your data, but they can be set by analyzing the actual outputs of the neural nets on the training data and, more importantly, on the test data. A walk-forward test must be performed using a data period not overlapping with the training data. During this process, the values of the three parameters will take shape.

### 7.4.2 Integrated pattern recognition

The integrated pattern recognition approach uses one neural net to identify all of the patterns. An output unit is assigned to each pattern you want to recognize (Figure 7.8). This approach seems more direct than the distributed approach, but the neural net required is much larger and more difficult to train than each of the smaller, distributed nets. The patterns for an integrated neural net are configured as follows: $x_1 x_2 x_3 \ldots x_A d_1 d_2 d_3 \ldots d_C$. If market pattern $i$ is being encoded, then $d_i$ is set to 1 and all other desired outputs are set to 0. The same selection algorithm can be used to interpret the results. Also, it is important to note that if a pattern is a subset of another (i.e. a double bottom is a subset of a triple bottom) then two desired outputs may be set to 1. In practice, double and triple tops and bottoms would not be selected for recognition in the same systems

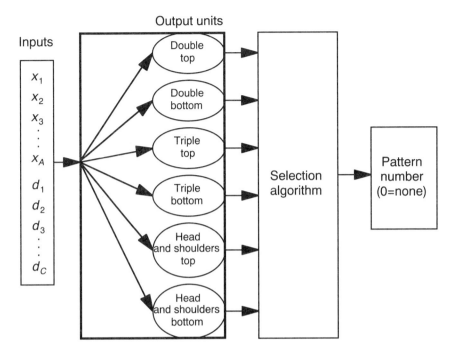

**Figure** 7.8 *Integrated pattern recognition.*

because of their inherent conflict. If you decide to include double tops/ bottoms in your approach, triple tops/bottoms will be detected early. If you select triple tops/bottoms in your approach, double tops/bottoms will go undetected.

The steps for building an integrated pattern recognition neural net are the same as for the distributed approach with the following exceptions (bold indicates differences from the distributed approach):

Step 1:  Locate the point in the data where each pattern is completed.
Step 2:  Build a pattern record for each of the points identified in step 1. Assign it to a pattern code from 1 to the number of patterns.
**Step 3:  Set desired output for pattern to detect to 1 and set all others to zero.**
**Step 4:  Train the neural net using the pattern records.**
Step 5:  Develop a selection algorithm.

Step 3 is required so that the correct output neuron has a high activity level when the target pattern is detected. Step 4, the training phase, is now only required for one net. The same selection algorithm can be used by simply substituting each output unit of the integrated neural net for the single output unit of each of the distributed neural nets.

## 7.5 Integrating technical indicators

Some technical indicators provide interesting features that can aid in the financial prediction accuracy. I have found that it is important to identify indicators that offer new information to the net, rather than just mathematical recombinations of the data. The neurons will provide all of the recombinations we will need. The key is to localize features that the neural net would otherwise have a hard time discerning. This approach is akin to providing the 'clues' to solve a mystery.

Some indicators that meet these requirements are RSI, Stochastic, MACD and ADX (Murphy, 1986). The RSI and the Stochastic indicators provide good insight into overbought/oversold conditions that help in detecting trend changes. The MACD and ADX indicators do not help in determining the direction of a market, but they do assist in detecting that a change is on the horizon.

Indicators can be used as input to a neural net using the same techniques previously described for price data. The overbought/oversold indicators, such as RSI and Stochastics, will not require normalization since their formulas already result in a fixed dynamic range. Because of this feature, providing the history of the indicator is not as significant as with the price data. An RSI value of 95 is considered overbought whether it was 90 yesterday or 100, although some technicians trade based only on patterns found in indicators. These traders place much more emphasis on a double bottom in an RSI value than they would on a double bottom in the price data. Again, you must experiment with various combinations of indicators and time frames to reach a solution that meets your needs.

## 7.6 Integrating related markets

For years traders have used data from related markets to help predict a particular target market. For example, bond, gold and dollar markets are all used to predict the stock market. Up to this point, we have concentrated on using one market for our analysis. By integrating data from other markets a neural net's performance can be enhanced (Ruggerio, 1994b). The easiest and probably the best way to integrate other markets into your neural net is simply to include the data as inputs to your net or apply indicators and use their outputs. The only hard and fast rule that I have found is that you must match the frequency of your data for all of the markets you would like to integrate. In other words, you cannot mix weekly bond data with daily S&P 500 data and expect the net to recognize the differing time periods. If you want to predict the S&P 500 and you are using daily data, you must also use daily data from the related market you want to integrate to enhance your performance.

Another way to improve your results is to use spreads. A spread is simply the difference between two related markets. The resulting graph of a spread lets a trader interpret the dynamic relationship between two markets to determine strength or weakness relative to each other. Various spreads can provide insight into future trend changes. For example, the spread between the Commodity Research Bureau (CRB) index (which is an index of commodity prices ands can be used as an inflation indicator) and the S&P 500 provides a spread that adjusts based on inflation. Thus, if the S&P 500 advances but the CRB index advances along with it, the result will be a flat spread. The spread may provide a critical piece of information that the net would otherwise be unable to learn. Spreads can be input to the neural net as a normalized snapshot of a particular point in time or they can be input as a window in recent history. Either way, you should take special care in only using spreads that have a significant impact on the market you are predicting and you should keep the amount of data to a minimum. If you decide to use the CRB index, you should not include gold as gold is a component of the CRB index. Some knowledge of the relationships between the markets you use is required to design an effective solution.

# 8

# Other trend prediction strategies

The more help you can give a neural net, the better job it will do predicting the future. This chapter describes some techniques that will help you help your neural nets. Sometimes, small variations to a particular method can produce significantly better results. Other times, performance can be adversely affected or improvements are negligible.

After you have been successful in developing a working neural net, you may want to experiment with the variations presented in this chapter. When conducting your experiments, it is important that you establish an analysis plan and carefully document your results. Your analysis plan should be based on incrementally adding, removing and combining various changes. This is especially important because you do not know exactly where all the pieces will fit together to make the optimal neural net trading system. The adding of a particular enhancement may have no effect on your results until you combine it with one or more other variations. Patience and good record keeping will go a long way towards finding a successful solution.

## 8.1 Sigmoid target calculation method

As described earlier, the target, or desired value, is the ideal value (or values) we would like a neural net's output units to produce, given a particular input pattern. The method used for target values was given previously by Equation 5.3.

$$d_i = \frac{c_i - c_{\text{low}}}{c_{\text{high}} - c_{\text{low}}}$$

This method is a linear technique that normalizes the targets in a range from a point in time when the market makes a relative low to when it makes a relative high.

In analyzing the systems generated with this approach, you can detect two primary problems:

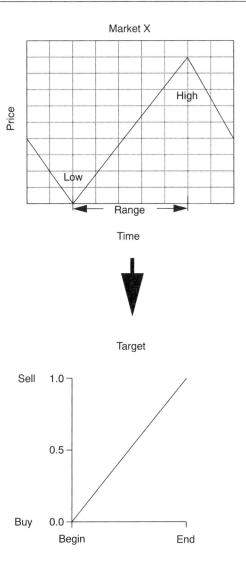

**Figure 8.1** *Linear target.*

1.  Signals are sometimes generated during minor retracements, causing the system to generate an early trend reversal.
2.  Signals are close to ideal points, but off by two or three days, causing less than ideal market entries.

The sigmoid target calculation method can help avoid these problems by emphasizing the target level at trend changes. Instead of using the linear target method shown in Figure 8.1, we will employ a target shape of an inverted sigmoid (Figure 8.2).

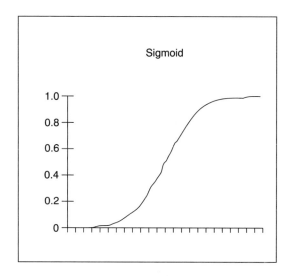

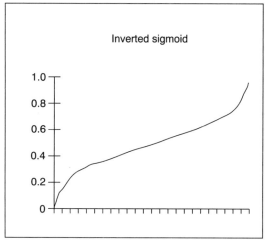

**Figure 8.2** *Sigmoid target.*

The sigmoid function is inverted (flipped) around the diagonal to provide the inverted sigmoid. This function, when applied to the standard target calculation equation, maintains target values at the end points while suppressing values near the end points. Values around the middle of the range remain almost unaffected. The patterns produced by this method trains the neural net to get excited only when a trend change pattern is present. This differs from the previous approach, which gradually provides a trend change signal.

To estimate the desired inverted sigmoid affect, the linear approach can be multiplied by a filter, as shown in Figure 8.3.

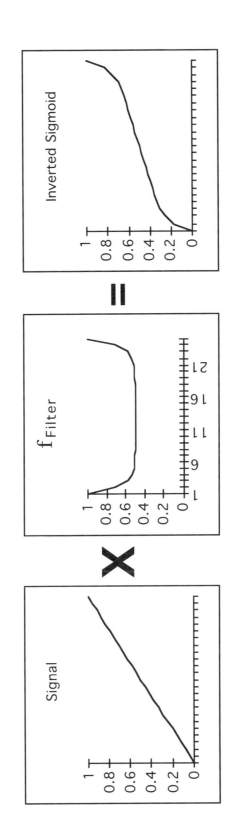

**Figure 8.3** *Signal transformation function.*

Equation 5.3 can be modified to produce the inverted sigmoid as shown in Equation 8.1.

$$d_i = \frac{c_i - c_{\text{low}}}{c_{\text{high}} - c_{\text{low}}} f_{\text{FILTER}}(i) \quad i = 1 \ldots N \tag{8.1}$$

The filter, when applied in this fashion, provides a good approximation of the shape desired and is easy to implement. Each discrete point is filtered relative to where the point falls within the range. The result is a series of values that are emphasized at the beginning and end of the range.

## 8.2 Selecting the optimum net configuration

In previous sections, some suggestions and guidelines have been presented for determining the configuration of your neural nets. The configuration of your net is totally dependent upon the patterns you want it to learn. For our purposes, the neural nets used are feed-forward, have one hidden layer and use sigmoid activation functions. Given these constants, the only configuration parameters left to be determined are the number of neurons needed in each layer.

The number of neurons in the input layer is easy to determine once you have selected the markets and the feature extraction approach to be used to train the net.

The output layer for generating a neural net indicator requires only one neuron driven to 0 when it is time to buy and to 1 when it is time to sell. Another approach to generating buy/sell signals is to use two neurons, one designated as the buy neuron and the other as the sell neuron (Figure 8.4). Ideally, the neurons will always mirror each other (as during training) so that the sum of the two neurons' outputs will equal 1. The primary advantage of this approach is that it has a built-in confirmation mechanism. When new patterns are presented to a net, the actual outputs are less than ideal. When one neuron signals, by reaching an acceptable threshold, the other neuron can be analyzed to confirm the signal and filter out bad signals.

By modifying the signal generation algorithm to include new threshold $t_{\text{BC}}$ and $t_{\text{SC}}$ (buy confirmation and sell confirmation respectively) the opposite neuron will have the final say. The confirmation threshold will be set to more conservative values than the signal thresholds, so as not to filter out good signals. The following provides an example of possible threshold values.

$t_{\text{S}} = 0.90$
$t_{\text{SC}} = 0.85$
$t_{\text{BC}} = 0.15$
$t_{\text{B}} = 0.10$

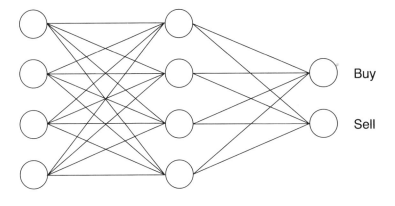

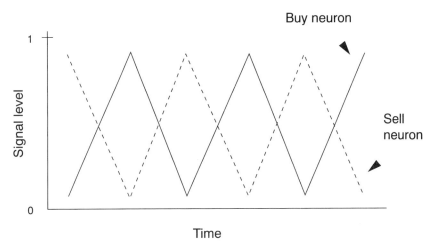

**Figure 8.4** *Two-neuron output layer.*

Given $0.05 \leqslant d \leqslant 0.95$.

The hidden layer is the most important layer to get right, and is also the most difficult. The neurons in the hidden layer are the real workhorse of the neural net. In Chapter 5, a technique was presented for estimating the number of neurons based on the number of patterns in the training set (Equations 5.4 and 5.5). Often this will provide an acceptable number of neurons, but I prefer to use this value as a starting point. If you see that your net does a great job learning the training set and the parameter set but fails on the test set, this usually means you have overestimated the number of neurons in your hidden layer. If your net does an acceptable job learning the training set and the parameter set but fails on the test set, this usually means you have too few neurons in your hidden layer. A good approach for optimizing the number of neurons in the hidden layer is called **pruning** and is based on analyzing a neuron's contribution to the solution. In fact, pruning can be applied to the entire neural net, except for the output layer. Simply take the magnitude ($m$) of all of the connections from a neuron to all of the neurons in the next layer; if $m$ is close to zero, then the neuron is not contributing to the solution and can be pruned (eliminated).

$$m(h_i) = \sum_{j=1}^{C} |w2_{ij}| \quad m(x_i) = \sum_{j=1}^{B} |w1_{ij}| \qquad (8.2)$$

The neural net has actually learned to ignore this neuron's output and is just taking up space in the net. In the example provided in Figure 8.5, we can easily see that the hidden neuron $h_1$ does not end up contributing to the solution as $w2_{11}$ is 0.02, which means that, no matter how active $h_1$ is, only 2% of its value will be sent to the output neuron. The same is true for input neuron $x_2$. All the weights from $x_2$ to the hidden layer are very close to zero, thereby severely dampening its effect on the net's final solution.

In order to use pruning effectively, the following algorithm can be used:

Step 1: Select B (the number of hidden neurons) based on the number of patterns in the training set.

Step 2: Train the net.

Step 3: Analyze the weights (Equation 8.2) and determine if pruning is possible. If pruning is possible, go to step 5.

Step 4: Increase the number of neurons by 25–50% and go to step 2. Care must be taken not to oscillate around the optimal solution. Stop if oscillation is detected.

Step 5: Prune the neurons that do not contribute to the solution. If an input neuron is pruned, then update the input patterns. Go to step 2.

## 8.3 Tailoring training to periodic data

The feature extraction window size is very important to the success or failure of your neural net. The selection of this parameter must be large enough to encompass sufficient data for learning, yet small enough so that insignificant data is not allowed to confuse the neural net. By uncovering the underlying period in the data, you can tailor the window size accordingly.

The dominant period will be used to set the window size. The dominant period is simply the period that occurs most often. To determine the period in the data, we will borrow from the percentage change technique

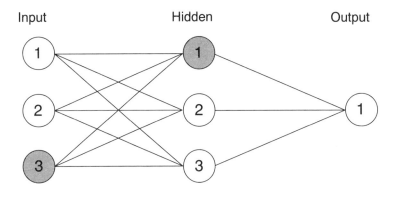

Hidden (*j*)

| $w1_{ij}$ | | 1 | 2 | 3 | *m* |
|---|---|---|---|---|---|
| Input (*i*) | 1 | −0.30 | 0.04 | 0.11 | 0.15 |
| | 2 | −0.01 | 0.03 | 0.02 | 0.02 |
| | 3 | −0.90 | −0.45 | 0.71 | 0.85 |

Output (*k*)

| $w2_{jk}$ | | 1 | *m*(*h*) |
|---|---|---|---|
| Hidden (*j*) | 1 | 0.02 | 0.02 |
| | 2 | −0.37 | 0.37 |
| | 3 | 0.62 | 0.62 |

**Figure 8.5** *Pruning example.*

used to determine the start and end of a signal (Chapter 5). A histogram can be built by counting the number of occurrences of each period length. Figure 8.6 is an example of a typical histogram.

From this example it is clear that a signal is usually generated every 16–21 days. A good window size is approximately one-half of the dominant period or, for the example, about nine days. This technique provides a good confirmation that the neural net is configured correctly.

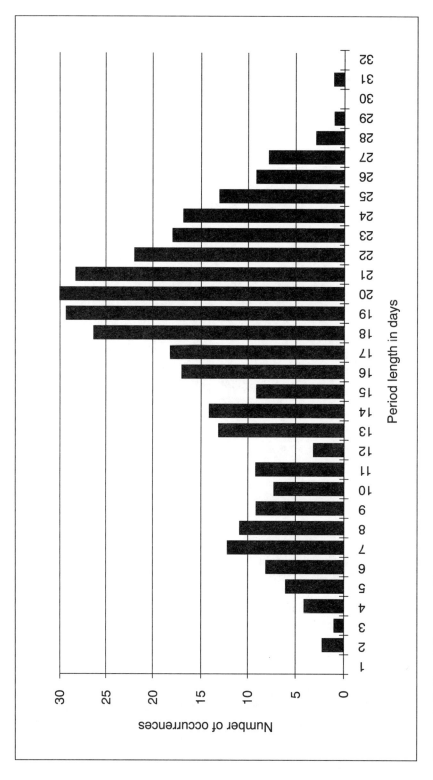

**Figure 8.6** *Signal frequency histogram.*

## 8.4 When is it time to retrain?

Eventually, all of your hard work will have to be repeated, but the question is, when? After a while, the data you used to train your neural net becomes older and older and there is more and more recent history that your neural net has not learned. It is impracticable and unprofitable to train every day. The generalizations that were made during the training period are valuable to making accurate predictions and constant training only serves to dilute the progress made. Of course, when the net gives a few bad predictions, you will be tempted to retrain, but that may not always be the best course of action. Every system has drawdowns and, as long as the results of your walk-forward testing are not exceeded, stick with the neural net. If you have exceeded the drawdown parameters, then a decision must be made. A good rule of thumb is: if 25% of your training set can be replaced by more recent data, then retrain. If you have exceeded your drawdown parameters and you do not have 25% new data to train on, then you should re-evaluate your entire neural net. In this case, there are more serious flaws that are causing the problems.

The feature extraction approach has focused on solving the dynamic range problem by converting absolute change into relative change. The major assumption of this approach is that the relative changes will be consistent over time and can therefore be used to predict the future. Market dynamics can change over the years and cause these relative changes to skew. One major change that has occurred in recent history is the incorporation of the up-tick rule on the New York Stock Exchange (NYSE). The NYSE, in the wake of the crash of 1987, instituted a new trading restriction when the Dow Jones Industrial Average (DJIA) advanced or declined by 50 or more points. When the DJIA drops by 50 points, sell orders can only be executed on an up-tick. When the DJIA advances by more than 50 points, buy orders can only be executed on a down-tick. On the days when this occurs, it may have the effect of adjusting the relative change in the market. A change in the market dynamics, like this one, could affect when a neural net should be retrained.

The other rule of thumb that you can use in conjunction with the 25% rule is based on the prediction term. Neural nets developed to produce long-term signals will need to be retrained less often than those developed for short-term signals. The two rules are related in that, if you have a short-term neural net, you should probably retrain when 10–15% of your data can be replaced. If you have a long-term neural net, then you may be able to wait until 35–40% of your data can be replaced.

# Part Three

## Price Prediction Techniques

# 9
# Basic strategy for price prediction

The objective of the price prediction approach is to predict the next day's price range accurately for the purpose of day trading. With this information, you can quickly profit from small, or sometimes large, daily fluctuation of a particular market. Day trading eliminates the overnight risk and is therefore a very desirable approach to trading. Overnight risk is the risk assumed by the investor when the market is closed (overnight, weekends and holidays). Major events that occur when the market is closed can significantly effect the opening price of the next day's trading session, causing a gap in the price data. A gap offers no opportunity to exit a position at the prices skipped over, which can cause greater than expected losses. By using a day trading approach, you are in and out of a trade in the same day and overnight risk is eliminated. The major disadvantage of a day trading approach is that you must be right a high percentage of the time, or have a very good money management system, in order to be profitable. A neural network can be used to increase your accuracy and overcome this disadvantage.

This chapter describes each of the steps required to build a price prediction system, as follows:

Step 1: feature extraction
Step 2: neural net configuration
Step 3: day trading algorithm
Step 4: training the net
Step 5: walk-forward testing.

## 9.1 Feature extraction

The strategy for creating input patterns for the day trading approach is to use the daily change in price ($\Delta$), as depicted in Table 9.1, to predict the next day's close, high and low.

Once a prediction is made for these three prices, different trading strategies can be implemented to apply the data. Each of the $\Delta$ values is normalized by using the same procedure as was used for the trend

**Table 9.1** Price prediction input pattern

| Neuron | $\Delta$ | = |
|--------|----------|---|
| 1 | $\Delta$Open | $o_{i+1} - c_i$ |
| 2 | $\Delta$Close$_1$ | $c_i - c_{i-1}$ |
| 3 | $\Delta$High$_1$ | $h_i - h_{i-1}$ |
| 4 | $\Delta$Low$_1$ | $l_i - l_{i-1}$ |
| 5 | $\Delta$Close$_2$ | $c_{i-1} - c_{i-2}$ |
| 6 | $\Delta$High$_2$ | $h_{i-1} - h_{i-2}$ |
| 7 | $\Delta$Low$_2$ | $l_{i-1} - l_{i-2}$ |
| 8 | $\Delta$Close$_3$ | $c_{i-2} - c_{i-3}$ |
| 9 | $\Delta$High$_3$ | $h_{i-2} - h_{i-3}$ |
| 10 | $\Delta$Low$_3$ | $l_{i-2} - l_{i-3}$ |

prediction approach. For each different type of $\Delta$ (open, close, high and low), the probable volatility window can be calculated by Equation 9.1.

$$\lambda = \frac{2}{P} \sum_{i=1}^{P} \frac{|\Delta|}{c_i} \qquad (9.1)$$

Then, each input to the net is calculated by Equation 9.2, replacing $\Delta$ with the appropriate entry from Table 9.1 and $\lambda$ with the appropriate probable volatility window value calculated for that $\Delta$.

$$x_i = \frac{\Delta}{c_i \lambda} \quad i = 1 \ldots A, \ -1 \leqslant x_i \leqslant 1 \qquad (9.2)$$

This linear approach forms a pattern from the previous three trading days using the change in price between consecutive days. One exception is the first $\Delta$ shown in Table 9.1. This $\Delta$ is the change between today's close and tomorrow's open. This may seem awkward, but it has the desired effect of increasing the accuracy of the prediction. The opening price of the day is very important because it represents the closing price from all overnight trading that has taken place. We are also guaranteed that this price will be in the trading range for the day. Some day trading systems only trade the first few hours of the day and base their strategy on whether the market opens up, down or flat.

We will train the neural net to learn which patterns precede rising prices and which patterns precede declining prices. To accomplish this we will need the close, high and low targets that provide the information we are looking for. We will calculate each of these targets as follows.

$$d_{1,i} = \frac{h_{i+1} - c_{i+1}}{c_i \lambda_h}$$

$$d_{2,i} = \frac{c_{i+1} - c_i}{c_i \lambda_c} \qquad (9.3)$$

$$d_{3,i} = \frac{c_{i+1} - l_{i+1}}{c_i \lambda_l}$$

The three desired outputs are normalized based on the probable volatility window and the closing price. As we are using a sigmoid activation function, we must also ensure that the desired outputs are positive and in the range of 0.05–0.95, so we will also apply the following finishing touches to the equation for calculating the desired outputs:

$$d_{1,i} = \min\left(\max\left(\frac{h_{i+1} - c_{i+1}}{c_i \lambda_h}, 0.05\right), 0.95\right)$$

$$d_{2,i} = \min\left(\max\left(\frac{c_{i+1} - c_i}{2c_i \lambda_c} + 0.5, 0.05\right), 0.95\right) \qquad (9.4)$$

$$d_{3,i} = \min\left(\max\left(\frac{c_{i+1} - l_{i+1}}{c_i \lambda_l}, 0.05\right), 0.95\right)$$

Note that $d_{2,i}$ is relative to the previous day's close and can be positive or negative; thus, it is compressed into the range of positive values from 0.05 to 0.95, where 0.5 indicates no change.

The desired output targets contain the information we want the net to learn, that is the next day's highest price, lowest price and closing price. If the results are correct, we can profit by placing a buy order near the low and a sell order near the high, or by placing a buy or sell at the open, depending upon whether the predicted close is above or below the opening price. After the training is completed, you can transform the net's outputs into predicted price levels by first predicting the close using Equation 9.5.

$$c_{i+1} = 2c_i\lambda_c(o_2 - 0.5) + c_i \qquad (9.5)$$

Then you can predict the high and low relative to the predicted close using Equation 9.6.

$$h_{i+j} = c_{i+1} + c_i \lambda_h o_1$$

$$l_{i+1} = c_{i+1} - c_i \lambda_l o_3 \qquad (9.6)$$

## 9.2 Neural net configuration

The number of input neurons in the price prediction net was determined based on the input data selected in Table 9.1. These 10 inputs characterize the preceding three days of price movement. The number of output units was determined to be 3, corresponding to the high, low and closing price we want to predict. The number of neurons in the hidden layer depends on the number and diversity of the input patterns. We can use the same formula as used in the trend prediction approach as follows:

$$B = \frac{\phi(248 - 10) - 3}{10 + 3 + 1} = \phi 17.0 - 0.214 \qquad \text{(Using 5.5)}$$

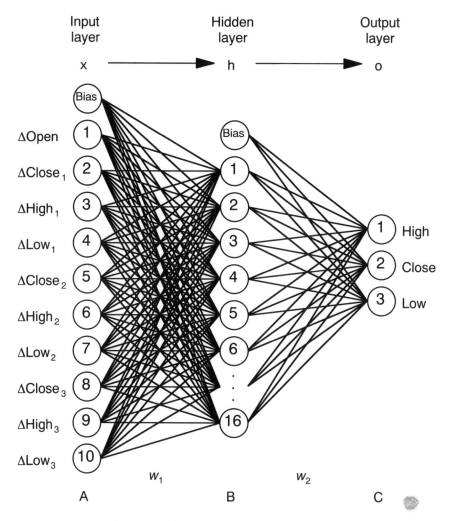

**Figure 9.1** *Neural net configuration for price prediction test case.*

If $\phi = 0.95$ then $B = 15.936 \approx 16$. We estimate that 16 neurons will be sufficient for the hidden layer if our $\phi$ assumption of 0.95 is correct. A high $\phi$ was selected because of the increased accuracy requirements of day trading. The neural net configuration for the price prediction approach is depicted in Figure 9.1.

## 9.3 Day trading algorithm

Before we can discuss the training phase, we must decide how we are going to use the neural net's predictions to trade. This is because various trading parameters must be finalized during the parameter phase of the training, so we must select those parameters before we start training. There are many different ways to day trade a market. For this basic strategy, I have selected an algorithm (Figure 9.2) that is easy to implement and can be tested with only daily data (open, high, low, close).

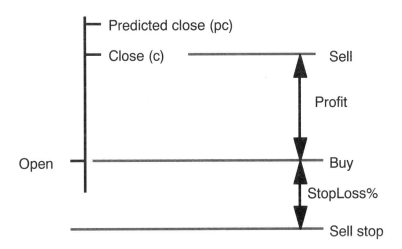

```
If Open < pc
        BUY LONG Open
        SELL Close
        STOP Open–(StopLoss% * Previous Close)
Else
        SELL SHORT Open
        BUY Close
        STOP Open+(StopLoss% * Previous Close)
Endif
```

**Figure 9.2** *Trading algorithm for price prediction.*

This algorithm works as follows. If the predicted close is higher than the opening price (open), then buy the open and sell the close at the end of the day. If the predicted close is lower than the opening price (open), then sell the open and buy the close at the end of the day. If the prediction is right, you will close the position at the end of the day and make a profit. You must also protect against being wrong, which will happen. To do this, you will place a stop loss order above or below your entry price based on a percentage of the previous day's close. If you are long, you will place a sell stop; if you are short, you will place a buy stop. We will call this parameter StopLoss%. The formulas for calculating your stop loss price are given by Equation 9.7.

$$\text{BuyStop} = o_{i+1} - c_i \, \text{StopLoss}\%$$
$$\text{SellStop} = o_{i+1} + c_i \, \text{StopLoss}\%$$

$$(9.7)$$

StopLoss% must be established during the parameter phase.

## 9.4 Training the net

The same time periods as used in Chapter 5 (1990–92) will be used to demonstrate the basic price prediction strategy. 1990 is the training set, 1991 is the parameter set and 1992 is the test set. The training of 1990 data will be accomplished using the back-propagation training algorithm. Accuracy is very important so a low tss is desired. Depending on the rules you establish for trading, various parameters must be resolved during the parameter phase. For the example, only StopLoss% will be established. A range of values for StopLoss% are applied until the profit is maximized and the drawdown is minimized. The midpoint of the range in which each parameter is maximized is then selected for use in the test phase.

## 9.5 Walk-forward testing

After you have completed the training and parameter phases, the walk-forward testing will provide the final test results. The trading algorithm is designed to generate only one trade per day. Other day trading algorithms, which will be discussed later, trade multiple times during the day. Using the basic price prediction strategy, the following results were obtained during the walk-forward period:

Profit: $16 355
Maxdraw: $10 105

$$\text{rprofit\%} = \frac{\$16\,355 \times 100}{\$5000 + (1.5 \times \$10\,105)} = 81\% \qquad \text{(Using 5.6)}$$

A minimum account size of only $5000 is required by many brokerage firms to day trade one S&P 500 futures contract. The lower requirement is because the risk of loss is minimized as the positions will not be held overnight. A commission plus slippage of $30 per trade was used. Using Equation 5.6, this system produced an annual return of 81%. In order to achieve this fantastic return, a 50% drawdown would have to be sustained, and this may not be easy to do. (The 50% drawdown is calculated by taking the maxdraw of $10 105 divided by initial account size of $20 200.) For this system, an initial account size of $30 000 may be more appropriate, depending upon your risk tolerance. This would reduce the drawdown to 34% and still produce a respectable 54.5% annual return.

## 9.6 Review of the basic strategy

Now that all of the details of the basic strategy have been defined, we can step through the process and generate some actual results. First you must calculate the probable volatility windows, the input patterns and the desired outputs. The probable volatility windows are calculated only for the training set data (1990). The values were calculated are as follows:

$$\lambda_o = 0.0069 \quad \lambda_h = 0.0131 \quad \lambda_l = 0.0150 \quad \lambda_c = 0.0157 \qquad (9.8)$$

These values are used throughout the remainder of the prediction. Next, the input patterns and desired outputs are calculated using Equations 9.2 and 9.4 respectively. The first 20 input patterns for 1990 are shown in Table 9.2.

Training is conducted with these patterns until the tss error reaches a plateau. Training was stopped after 600 epochs with a final tss of 61.7, as shown in Figure 9.3. Some patterns are learned better than others, as can be seen in Figure 9.4.

The next step is to run the parameter set patterns (1991) through the net using the weights learned from training 1990 and record the actual outputs for each pattern. The actual outputs are then transformed into predicted prices using Equations 9.5 and 9.6. The day trading algorithm is applied to these predicted prices for a range of StopLoss% values as shown in Figure 9.5.

By analyzing these results, you can see that the profitable range for StopLoss% is from 0.14 to 0.24. The midpoint of this range (0.19) is selected as the StopLoss% to be used in the walk-forward test. Figure 9.6 contains the results from the walk-forward period (1992).

As you can see, StopLoss% = 0.19 was very profitable, but it was not the best. The is normally the case with walk-forward testing, and you should not be tempted to use parameters that are not close to the middle

**Table 9.2** Excerpt from a price prediction pattern file (1990)

| Date | $x_1$ Open | $x_2$ Close | $x_3$ High | $x_4$ Low | $x_5$ Close | $x_6$ High | $x_7$ Low | $x_8$ Close | $x_9$ High | $x_{10}$ Low | $d_1$ High | $d_2$ Close | $d_3$ Low |
|---|---|---|---|---|---|---|---|---|---|---|---|---|---|
| 19900108 | -0.169 | -0.867 | 0.950 | 0.052 | -0.306 | 0.547 | 0.650 | -0.132 | 0.616 | 0.069 | 0.169 | 0.744 | 0.685 |
| 19900109 | 0.093 | 0.484 | 0.168 | 0.679 | -0.861 | 0.950 | 0.052 | -0.303 | 0.543 | 0.645 | 0.950 | 0.062 | 0.052 |
| 19900110 | -0.113 | -0.889 | 0.950 | 0.052 | 0.490 | 0.170 | 0.689 | -0.873 | 0.950 | 0.052 | 0.380 | 0.425 | 0.802 |
| 19900111 | 0.454 | -0.150 | 0.381 | 0.804 | -0.891 | 0.950 | 0.052 | 0.491 | 0.170 | 0.690 | 0.331 | 0.546 | 0.175 |
| 19900112 | -0.950 | 0.091 | 0.330 | 0.175 | -0.150 | 0.381 | 0.803 | -0.890 | 0.950 | 0.052 | 0.950 | 0.001 | 0.192 |
| 19900115 | 0.097 | -0.950 | 0.950 | 0.198 | 0.094 | 0.340 | 0.180 | -0.154 | 0.392 | 0.827 | 0.515 | 0.350 | 0.081 |
| 19900116 | -0.950 | -0.301 | 0.518 | 0.081 | -0.950 | 0.950 | 0.199 | 0.095 | 0.342 | 0.181 | 0.186 | 0.749 | 0.950 |
| 19900117 | 0.155 | 0.495 | 0.185 | 0.950 | -0.299 | 0.514 | 0.081 | -0.950 | 0.950 | 0.197 | 0.950 | 0.214 | 0.161 |
| 19900118 | -0.684 | -0.577 | 0.950 | 0.163 | 0.500 | 0.187 | 0.950 | -0.301 | 0.518 | 0.081 | 0.083 | 0.681 | 0.877 |
| 19900119 | 0.642 | 0.360 | 0.082 | 0.872 | -0.574 | 0.950 | 0.162 | 0.497 | 0.186 | 0.950 | 0.206 | 0.616 | 0.144 |
| 19900122 | -0.077 | 0.230 | 0.205 | 0.143 | 0.358 | 0.082 | 0.869 | -0.572 | 0.950 | 0.161 | 0.950 | 0.001 | 0.197 |
| 19900123 | 0.950 | -0.950 | 0.950 | 0.203 | 0.237 | 0.212 | 0.148 | 0.369 | 0.085 | 0.894 | 0.950 | 0.399 | 0.065 |
| 19900124 | -0.950 | -0.203 | 0.950 | 0.065 | -0.950 | 0.950 | 0.204 | 0.238 | 0.212 | 0.148 | 0.138 | 0.751 | 0.950 |
| 19900125 | 0.357 | 0.499 | 0.137 | 0.950 | -0.201 | 0.950 | 0.064 | -0.950 | 0.950 | 0.202 | 0.950 | 0.001 | 0.138 |
| 19900126 | 0.303 | -0.950 | 0.950 | 0.140 | 0.507 | 0.139 | 0.950 | -0.205 | 0.950 | 0.065 | 0.793 | 0.504 | 0.859 |
| 19900129 | 0.485 | 0.009 | 0.793 | 0.859 | -0.950 | 0.950 | 0.140 | 0.507 | 0.139 | 0.950 | 0.547 | 0.491 | 0.691 |
| 19900130 | 0.202 | -0.018 | 0.547 | 0.691 | 0.009 | 0.793 | 0.859 | -0.950 | 0.950 | 0.140 | 0.579 | 0.366 | 0.831 |
| 19900131 | 0.731 | -0.268 | 0.581 | 0.835 | -0.018 | 0.549 | 0.694 | 0.009 | 0.797 | 0.863 | 0.032 | 0.950 | 0.835 |
| 19900201 | 0.120 | 0.934 | 0.032 | 0.823 | -0.264 | 0.573 | 0.823 | -0.018 | 0.541 | 0.684 | 0.265 | 0.465 | 0.222 |
| 19900202 | -0.400 | -0.071 | 0.265 | 0.222 | 0.935 | 0.032 | 0.824 | -0.265 | 0.573 | 0.824 | 0.319 | 0.712 | 0.685 |

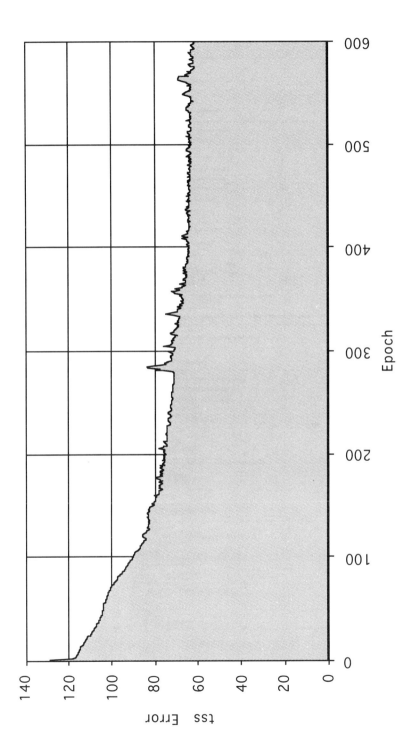

**Figure 9.3** *Graph of tss error for the test case training period (1990).*

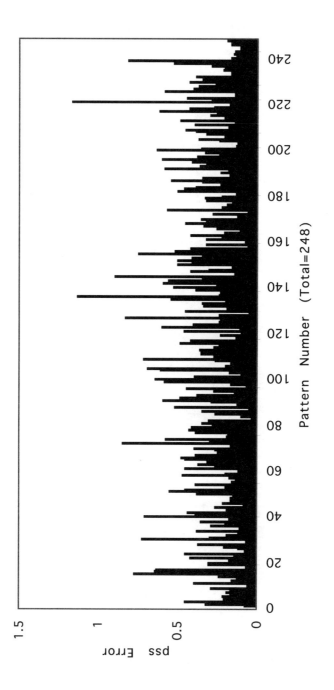

**Figure 9.4** *Graph of pss error/pattern for the test case training period (1990).*

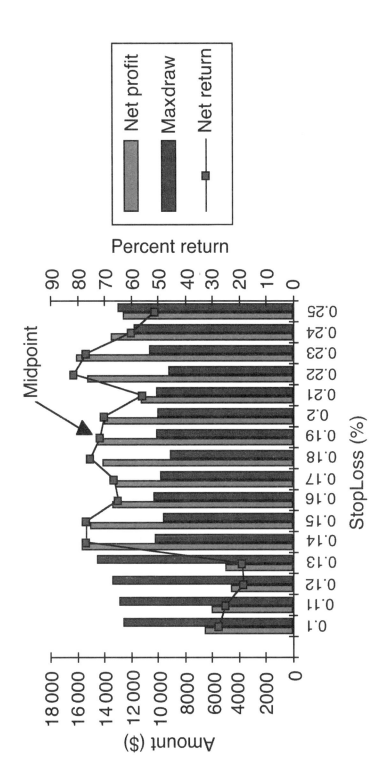

Figure 9.5 *Results of 1991 parameter phase.*

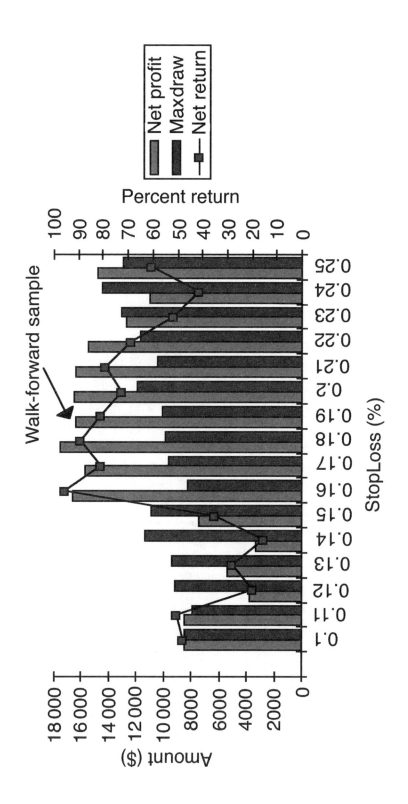

Figure 9.6 *Results of 1992 walk-forward testing.*

of the profitable range. For example, if you decided to take the highest net profit from the parameter set (StopLoss% = 0.23), then your results in the walk-forward period would have been severely affected. By staying near the middle, your system can withstand the prediction errors that will be encountered.

# 10
# Advanced feature extraction techniques for price prediction

Many of the techniques described in this chapter are similar to the ones presented in Chapter 7 for trend prediction. I will point out the differences in their application, but the implementation details are the same as presented in Chapter 7 and so will not be repeated here.

## 10.1 Range compression

The range compression techniques presented in Chapter 7 can also be used in price prediction. The exponential or Fibonacci techniques are helpful in providing overall trend data to the price prediction net. Various trading patterns will demonstrate different results depending upon the trend they exist in. By using range compression you can give your net a good indication of the prevailing trend, without overloading it with useless data. For example, using the example used to present the basic approach in Chapter 9, we could add additional input neurons based on the Fibonacci sequence. Given that the last three days are encoded in the existing neurons, these new neurons could represent the previous eight-, 13- and 21-day differences in closing prices. In other words, the data during these periods can be averaged and the difference between their average and the current closing price would provide a good indication of the trend.

## 10.2 Using logarithms

In Chapter 9, all of the examples were based on calculating differences. The same basic approach can be modified to use ratios and then calculate the net inputs based on the log of the ratios. Table 9.1 can be replaced by Table 10.1 to apply this approach.

## 10.3 Pattern recognition

The same basic approach as used for trend prediction can be used for price prediction, except the time frame is shorter. The shape extraction

**Table 10.1** Price prediction input pattern using log(ratios)

| Neuron | $\Delta$ | = log( ) |
|--------|----------|----------|
| 1 | $\Delta$Open | $o_{i+1}/c_i$ |
| 2 | $\Delta$Close$_1$ | $c_i/c_{i-1}$ |
| 3 | $\Delta$High$_1$ | $h_i/h_{i-1}$ |
| 4 | $\Delta$Low$_1$ | $l_i/l_{i-1}$ |
| 5 | $\Delta$Close$_2$ | $c_{i-1}/c_{i-2}$ |
| 6 | $\Delta$High$_2$ | $h_{i-1}/h_{i-2}$ |
| 7 | $\Delta$Low$_2$ | $l_{i-1}/l_{i-2}$ |
| 8 | $\Delta$Close$_3$ | $c_{i-2}/c_{i-3}$ |
| 9 | $\Delta$High$_3$ | $h_{i-2}/h_{i-3}$ |
| 10 | $\Delta$Low$_3$ | $l_{i-2}/l_{i-3}$ |

technique is especially useful for price prediction. It is recommended that no change threshold be used, as our horizon is so short that we do not want to mask price changes that could affect our results.

## 10.4 Integrating other data

The same ideas used for integrating technical indicators and related markets can be applied to price prediction. The indicators must be tailored to the shorter time periods and contain information that the net would otherwise be unable to extract from the existing input data. Longer periods can be used in the indicators to provide trend data, which can be very helpful to the net. The related markets used must be timely and have a direct impact on the price. They must also be synchronized to the frequency of the data to be useful.

## 10.5 Multiple period integration

Multiple period integration (MPI) is a technique whereby multiple price predictions are output from the different nets, all using a different time horizon. The results of each net are analyzed to determine the trading strategy for the upcoming day. The basic approach could be one of these nets. Other nets can be developed using range compression, pattern recognition and different time periods, all of which produce variations in the predictions. The difficult part of this approach is determining how to use the new data. The most basic approach is simply to average the results of all of the nets. For example, if we developed a system of three nets, we could average the predicted closes of all of them to arrive at a final prediction. But, what if the predicted closes varied significantly? We could end up ruining a good prediction by averaging with a bad one. A better approach is to first compare the results and develop an algorithm (or an expert system) for interpreting the results. For example, if two of the results were very close to each other and the third was far away, we could assume that the first two results are better and just average them and discard the third result. A more stringent approach is to require all of the results to be within a certain error tolerance. If the criterion is not met, then no trading takes place.

# 11
# Other price prediction strategies

## 11.1 Using a SOM for price prediction

The qualities of a SOM make it ideally suited for price prediction strategies (Glazier, 1990; Caudill, 1993). Two approaches are provided, one based on using supervised training and the other based on unsupervised training.

### 11.1.1 Supervised SOM for price prediction

The supervised approach is based on grouping patterns that produce the same change in price. An output neuron is assigned to each range of price changes to be identified, including two neurons to represent greater than a maximum and less than a minimum.

As shown in Figure 11.1, the SOM will classify all of the patterns that fit into the predefined ranges by forcing the appropriate neuron to be the winner. Also included is a neuron that represents the unchanged or, more accurately, almost unchanged state (−0.1 to +0.1%). After the SOM supervised training process is completed, new patterns can be presented to the SOM and the corresponding output neuron will be active. The key to interpreting the results is continuity. If one neuron is noticeably higher than all the rest, then we have a clear signal. If two or more neurons are significantly active, then additional interpretation is required. A good approach to analyzing multiple signals is to ignore signals when they are not occurring in contiguous neurons. If neurons 2 and 7 are active, then it is obvious that the SOM is not able to classify the pattern. A nice way to see what is happening is to present the results in the form of a graph.

Figure 11.2a clearly shows that the SOM predicts a down day. Figure 11.2b portrays a very different picture. Here we can see that multiple neurons are active, which indicates that the SOM is unable to classify this pattern and we should therefore refrain from trading. Also, Figure 11.2c is a clear buy signal, as indicated by the spike in the 0.3–0.5% range neuron.

In order to make this information useful, a trading strategy must be developed. A simple strategy would be to buy when neurons in the positive ranges are active, sell when neurons in the negative ranges are active

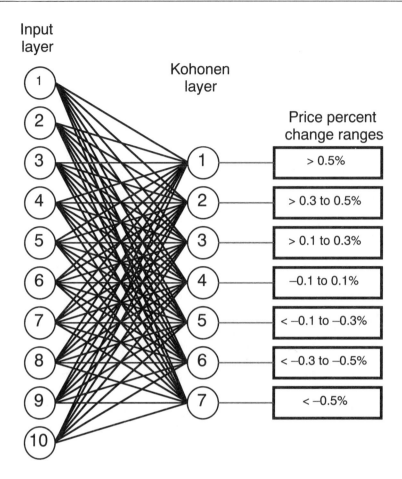

**Figure 11.1** *SOM for price prediction (supervised).*

and stand aside when neutral or conflicting activations occur. Another approach is to use the price percent change information to your advantage. For example, if you receive a prediction generated by the 0.3–0.5% range neuron, then you can use that to trade, based on the opening price of the day. The active neuron becomes the exit point of a long or a short position. The real indication of whether or not a trade is entered is based on the difference between the opening price and the active neuron's price range. Obviously, if the open is in the range then little or no profit potential exists.

### 11.1.2 Unsupervised SOM for price prediction

When using an unsupervised SOM, we are depending upon the SOM to find the classes that exist within the data. To implement this approach,

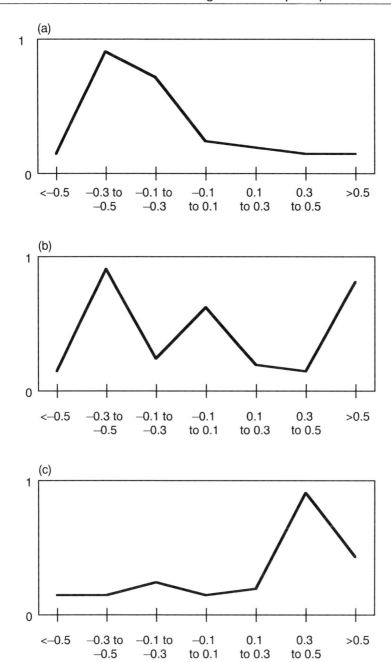

**Figure** 11.2 *Example graphs of supervised SOM results.*

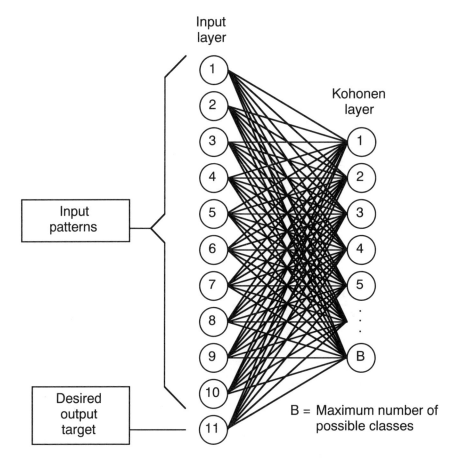

**Figure 11.3** *SOM for price prediction (unsupervised).*

the targets that were used to determine the winning neuron in the supervised approach are included in the input patterns (Figure 11.3).

Now the unsupervised algorithm is performed and similar patterns are assigned to the same output neuron. Unfortunately, the same historical pattern will generate different winning neurons and different patterns will activate the same neuron. To resolve these conflicts, we will analyze the group of patterns assigned to each neuron. The ones that have the lowest deviation in percent price change predictions will be the tradable patterns. In effect, what has been accomplished is that we have determined which patterns exhibit the highest probability of producing consistent results. The higher the probability, the higher the chance that a profitable trade can be realized.

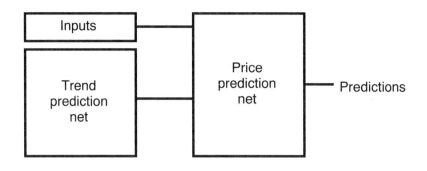

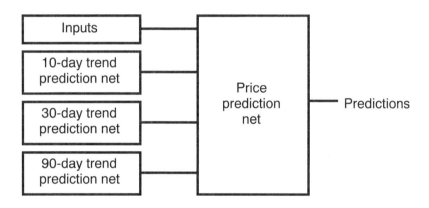

Figure 11.4 *Using a trend predictor as input to a price predictor.*

## 11.2 Combining position trading with day trading

The two basic approaches that have been presented in this book provide valuable information that can be integrated with each other. The combination of the two strategies can improve your results. For instance, the trend direction output from a trend prediction net can assist in determining which side of the market would provide the most effective entry point in a day trading system. Conversely, the outputs of a price prediction net can be used to set the stop loss prices for a position trading system.

When designing a day trading system, an indication of the long-term and short-term trends can assist the net in deciphering conflicting data. The net developed for trend prediction generates just the right output to feed to a day trading net to provide this information. This reduces the number of inputs that must be learned by the day trading net, which decreases training time and increases the accuracy of the predictions. Figure 11.4 provides a simple example of how this can be accomplished.

You can also have multiple trend prediction nets to provide various trend durations. As shown in Figure 11.4, long-term, intermediate and short-term trend predictors can be especially useful. The selection of your time horizons can be critical, and much experimentation is required to determine the right mix. Most markets exhibit cycles in multiples of three- or 10 day periods, so these time frames are common in technical analysis.

When developing the trading strategy for the position trading system, we used a fixed, dollar amount, StopLoss. The selection of this amount significantly affects the profit results. A price prediction net tailored to predict only daily highs and lows would be extremely helpful in this area. The high/low predictor could be used to adjust the stops of a position trading system on a daily or weekly basis. The daily predictions, plus or minus a cushion factor, could provide a tight stop that can protect profits and cut losses short.

## 11.3 Intraday neural net strategies

The day trading strategies presented in previous chapters all concentrated on predicting a 'trading range' each day and then using that information to make one trade that day. This approach may be applicable to some traders, but other full-time traders will want to take advantage of the numerous intraday fluctuations in a market. The first hurdle that must be overcome is the acquisition of the data. In order to trade multiple times within a single day, you must have real-time data and be able to react quickly. Data providers will transmit every tick and can usually draw a chart in front of you, in real time, based on the chart parameters you select. For our discussions, we will use five-minute bars. Five-minute bars look just like a daily open-high-low-close bar, but the data used to generate it is only for the last five minutes of trading. What you will quickly realize is that the five-minute chart looks very similar to the daily chart, only the time horizon has changed. We can therefore use a neural net in the same way as for position trading, but with some modifications in the training process and the trading algorithm.

The normal S&P 500 futures contract trading day is from 9.30 a.m. to 4:15 p.m. EST, for 6.75 hours of trading each day. This can be subdivided into 81 five-minute periods, which can be analyzed by the neural net. The same neural net used for the position trading test case (Figure 5.3) can be used for intraday trading, except for the number of hidden units, which will be discussed later. The output of this net will be an indicator, specifically tuned to day trading. The same major step (as used in position trading) will be required:

- feature extraction
- neural net configuration
- training the net
- signal generation
- walk-forward testing.

For each day, the ideal buy and sell points are detected by the feature extraction process. The patterns generated by these points are then used to initiate buy and sell signals associated with the corresponding desired output targets. The net is trained, the signal generation parameters are established and then the walk-forward testing can be performed to determine if the developed net is profitable. The whole process can mirror the trend prediction process, with the following variations. As a minimum of 10 five-minute periods will be required to build the first possible pattern for each day, trading cannot begin earlier than 50 minutes into the trading day, or 10:20 a.m. Also, as we are day trading, a new trade should not be established too late in the day, such as after 3:30 p.m. When a signal is generated after 3:30 p.m., the current position should simply be closed out. If no signal is received by 4:10 p.m., five minutes before the close, the current position should be closed, to avoid an overnight trade. Each time a signal is received, you must reverse your position. In other words, if you are long 10 contracts and you received a sell signal, you must sell 20 contracts to be net short 10 contracts. These trades must be placed quickly and be market orders.

The major disadvantage of this approach is the enormous amount of data that must be processed. Each day, 70 patterns will be generated. If we limit the training to only the last 20 trading days, we still have 1400 patterns to learn! That is significant when compared with the 252 patterns using in the position trading approach. Using Equation 5.5, an estimated 58 hidden units will be required. This net will require a long training period and may have difficulty converging on an acceptable solution. The trade-offs that must be evaluated are data time interval, the number of input neurons and the number of historical trading days. The optimum combination of these parameters will require numerous simulations to determine the right mix.

A second approach to intraday trading is to build a neural net to predict the price some number of periods in the future and then use that prediction to determine the appropriate trade. Still using five-minute periods, we could train a net to predict the price five and 10 periods in the future (25–50 minutes). When both predictions are greater that an acceptable distance from the current price, a signal is generated. To determine when to close a position, both predictions can be depicted graphically and, when they cross each other, an alert can be generated that warns the trader that the position should be closed soon. If the predictions are accurate, they will start to reverse as the price continues towards the prediction. When the price reverses direction after the alert, the position is closed. For example, if the current price is 500 and the five-period prediction is 550 and the 10-period prediction is 575, the system would generate a buy signal. Then, some time in the future, if the 10-period prediction fell to 540 and the five-period prediction stayed at 550, an alert would be generated. Then, if the price advanced to 570 and then declined to 555 the next period, a sell would be executed to close the position for a 55-point profit. This is one of many scenarios that can exist, and there are many different approaches to handling these conditions, for example limit orders can be used at the predicted levels, trailing stops a fixed distance behind the price and a crossover of the prediction and the price can be used.

# Part Four

## The Future of Neural Nets for Financial Prediction

# 12
# Integrating with other branches of artificial intelligence

All of the discussions in this book have intentionally focused on one branch of AI, neural networks. Much research has been done using other AI techniques, such as expert systems, fuzzy logic and genetic algorithms. This chapter explores how neural nets can be used in conjunction with these other techniques to increase the performance of a trading system.

## 12.1 Expert systems

A knowledge-based expert system uses human experiences in a specific application domain to make decisions based on a given repository of data (Felsen, 1990; Glazier, 1990; Stein, 1991b). The human experiences are normally of individuals thought to be experts in their related field. The primary motivation for developing an expert system is to encapsulate the expert's knowledge so that it can be repeated in the decision-making process or be used to train others in the same field of knowledge. The experts determine the rules necessary to make decisions based on the input data and then these rules are encoded into the system (Figure 12.1).

The heart of the expert system is the inference engine. The rules and the data are fed to the inference engine, which matches them up to form a conflict set. Each time through the inference engine loop, one rule is selected and executed. The loop continues until a trading decision is reached or the conflict set is empty, in which case no decision can be made. The expert system approach allows the combination of many different rules, from various experts, to be combined to form a trading system that should outperform any one individually. For example, some traders have specific rules for trading near holidays. History has shown that the markets tend to advance the day before and after certain holidays. These rules can be combined with rules that we used for making our neural net trading decisions, plus other rules that have been documented in numerous textbooks. Theoretically, the end result will be a super trading expert, but the careful planning and selection of the rules is critical to the success of the system. Too many disperse and conflicting rules may cause the system to miss good trading opportunities.

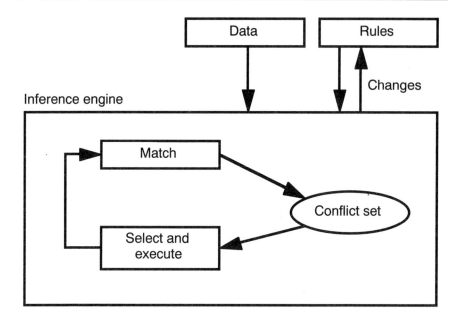

**Figure 12.1** *Expert system. (Glazier, 1990. Copyright © 1990, Technical Analysis, Inc. Used with permission.)*

Integrating a neural net into an position trading expert system is actually quite straightforward. The data is the output of the neural net and the rules are the same as the signal generation rules defined in Chapter 5. The data and rules can be combined with other data, fuzzy logic and rules to form a robust trading system.

## 12.2 Genetic algorithms

Genetic algorithms are a very interesting branch of AI owing to their relatively simplistic approach and their strong capabilities. A genetic algorithm (GA) determines the solution to a given problem by representing the problem in terms of genetic evolution (Burke, 1993). Different solutions are treated as distinct individuals in an evolving population. The individuals who best solve the problem at hand are determined to be the **fittest**. Borrowing from the Darwinian theory of **survival of the fittest**, the strongest (best) individuals are more likely to survive and, thus, procreate. The offspring, which are created by combining the chromosomes of its parents, become new solutions to the problem. Weaker individuals that do not meet the minimum acceptable criteria will die, and some will mutate into a different individual. The evolutionary process continues until the best individual produces an acceptable solution.

Genetic algorithms are used to solve problems in the form $\vec{y} = f(\vec{x})$ by treating the input vector ($\vec{x}$) like the chromosome of an individual in an evolving genetic system. The output vector ($\vec{y}$) represents the features of each individual (solution to the problem). These features are evaluated based on the rules of a particular society and are determined to be fit, unfit, or something in between. The fittest survive and mate with others in the population and the unfit die. Mutation can also occur, whereby a selected offspring's chromosome is modified in a random manner to allow varied solutions to evolve. The fitness determination is called the **merit function**. When the merit function of one or more individuals is in the acceptable range, the problem has been solved. The development of a good merit function is critical to the GA's success.

The algorithm repetitively cycles through generations of the population until the merit of one or more individuals is in the acceptable range. The methods used for computing the merit function and the algorithms used for mating, dying and mutating all vary depending upon the application. A critical component of a GA is the mating function, as this determines how new solutions to the problem are generated. The most common mating algorithm is the crossover algorithm. This technique divides two individuals' chromosomes into sections and then swaps their genes based on these divisions, creating two new offspring. Other important variables must also be resolved, including how to create the initial population (genesis) and how to control the population size. The selection and maintenance of the algorithm's parameters can significantly affect its performance.

A GA can be used to make trading decisions by developing chromosomes from historical price data, similar to the way in which the price data was preprocessed for a neural net. Then, two merit functions can be developed: one for a buy signal and one for a sell signal. Two separate genetic evolutions can then take place and the algorithm will find the solution that produces the best results, according to how the merit functions are designed. A GA can also be used in place of the back-propagation training algorithm to train a neural net. The weights of the neural net become the chromosomes and the merit function rewards individuals of the population that produce solutions with low errors.

# 13
# Getting started

There are many hurdles, most very tedious, that one must overcome in order to get off the ground toward developing a neural net-based trading system. This chapter will assist the reader in taking those first steps and provide some pointers along the way.

## 13.1 Selecting an approach

How you apply neural nets will depend upon your specific goals and your access to the resources necessary to accomplish them. This book has focused on using the S&P 500 futures contract to demonstrate various methods, but, this investment vehicle may be too speculative for the average investor. Possibly mutual funds, individual stocks or bonds would be more appropriate for your particular needs. The best way to get started is to pick a market of which you have had some experience. If you have been holding a mutual fund for a few years and are not happy with its performance, try starting there. Also, you should be sure you can get access to the data for a reasonable amount of time and money.

## 13.2 Acquiring market data

Market data is now available everywhere you turn. If you pick up any issue of *Technical Analysis of Stocks and Commodities* or *Futures* magazine, you will find may vendors willing to sell you preformatted, verified data at relatively low prices. It is important that the data is accurate, otherwise you may be training your neural net on invalid information. Make sure the data is compatible with the system you are going to be using. I use Microsoft Visual Basic and comma-separated value (CSV) files, which are easy to read into any spreadsheet or application program. Some vendors also sell charting and analysis programs with their data. This may be convenient, but it is not a requirement for developing your neural net system. The following companies have advertised in recent publications: Bonneville Market Information, CSI, Data Broadcasting Corporation, Data Transmission Network, Knight-Ridder Financial Publications, Pinnacle

Data Corp., S&P Comstock, Technical Tools, Tick Data, Inc. and Worden Brothers, Inc. Another very important factor you should consider when determining how you will acquire your market data is how you will keep it current. Some vendors offer real-time data or end-of-day updates. This will depend on the type of system you develop and the number of markets you will track. If you decide to develop only an S&P 500 system, then you may not need an additional service after you have your initial batch of data. From that point on, you could enter the data manually each day from newspaper or other on-line services. If you are tracking multiple markets or are day trading multiple times within a day, then a full-featured data service will probably be required. Remember that, if you decide to enter the data manually, you will make errors so you should have some basic error checking built into your system. If can be as simple as comparing highs and lows or you can compute standard deviations and generate warnings when the market fluctuates outside normal ranges. You must also decide how much data you will need. I have used anywhere from three to 10 years of S&P 500 data to train various neural nets. The primary rule is start small and keep it simple. Add the complexity only if you are not satisfied with the results.

## 13.3 Sticking to your system

After all is said and done, the hardest part is to actually do what your neural net predictor is telling you to do. That may seem ridiculous, but I have seen it happen many times. Once you start being successful, your human intuition kicks in and you start to think you are better than the neural net. The worst thing that can happen is to be successful at deviating from the system. Then it becomes even more difficult to get back on track.

The first thing you must realize is that trading stirs emotions. You can be elated when you make a successful trade and depressed when you have lost. I have found that the key to being successful is to match the system that you develop to your personality. If you cannot tolerate your portfolio being down 20% on your way to a 50% return, then modify your system or your money management techniques to accommodate that fact. The other important factor you should keep fresh in your mind is the expected results of your system. If during your walk-forward testing you consistently experience a 25% drawdown and you are currently at 20%, don't panic! You are within the parameters that your system predicted. But also realize when you have exceeded those parameters and it is time to stop the train. It is always better to stop and analyze the problems when your system is not performing the way you expected and have the capital to come back and trade another day.

## 13.4 Conclusions

At this point you should have a good appreciation of the amount of research and experimentation that is required to integrate neural nets into your market analysis application effectively. I hope that the methods and techniques presented have helped you in some way and have also sparked new ideas that will lead to better ways of analyzing your data. This book has intentionally limited its focus to just a few types of neural nets and has only touched on other areas of AI. This approach was selected so that end-to-end coverage of what it takes to build, test and implement neural net trading systems could be provided. Further research in the application of expert systems, fuzzy logic, genetic algorithms and other types of neural nets could provide improvements and refinements to future systems.

You now have all the information you need to get started. One final word of advice is to take small steps and document everything you do, even the failures. Keep track of what worked as well as what did not work. Log all of the neural net training sessions, the walk-forward results and the final system results for a wide range of parameters. I have found that having this data saves a great deal of time and, more importantly, builds confidence in the final system.

# Appendix A
## Back-propagation algorithm

The back-propagation algorithm gets its name from the manner in which it trains the neural net. It determines the error of the net's outputs when compared with desired outputs and propagates that error back through the network, adjusting each weight based on its associated error. This appendix contains the derivation of the equations that are used to update the weights on each pass through the algorithm (Rumelhart *et al.*, 1986; McClelland and Rumelhart, 1988; Carpenter and Hoffman, 1995), followed by a straightforward algorithm that can be used to implement back-propagation in the language of your choice (Knight, 1990).

The forward pass begins by presenting input vectors to the network. The total input to a neuron is calculated by Equation A.1:

$$x_j = \sum_i y_i \, w_{ji} \qquad (A.1)$$

A unit's output can then be calculated by using the sigmoid activation function:

$$y_j = \frac{1}{1 + e^{-x_j}} \qquad (A.2)$$

The goal of the algorithm is to find a set of weights such that the outputs generated by each input vector match, or are sufficiently close to, the desired output vector. First we will need to calculate the total error generated by the network:

$$E = \frac{1}{2} \sum_c \sum_j (y_{j,c} - d_{j,c})^2 \qquad (A.3)$$

where $c$ is the number of input/output vector pairs and $j$ is the number of output units. The forward pass is now complete and the backward pass can begin. The first step of the backward pass is to calculate $\delta E/\delta y$ for each output unit. By differentiating Equation A.3 we get:

$$\frac{\partial E}{\partial y_j} = y_j - d_j \qquad (A.4)$$

The chain rule can then be used to get $\partial E/\delta x$:

$$\frac{\partial E}{\partial x_j} = \frac{\partial E}{\partial y_j} \cdot \frac{dy_j}{dx_j} \qquad (A.5)$$

We now need to differentiate Equation A.2 to get $dy_j/dx_j$ and by substitution we get:

$$\frac{\partial E}{\partial x_j} = \frac{\partial E}{\partial y_j} \cdot y_j(1 - y_j) \qquad (A.6)$$

At this point we know how the error will be affected by a change in the input, so now we need to compute how a change in the weights will affect the error. For any weight $w_{ij}$, from $i$ to $j$ the derivative is:

$$\frac{\partial E}{\partial w_{ji}} = \frac{\partial E}{x_j} \cdot \frac{\partial x_j}{\partial w_{ji}} = \frac{\partial E}{x_j} \cdot y_j \qquad (A.7)$$

So the effect on the output is:

$$\frac{\partial E}{\partial x_j} \cdot \frac{\partial x_j}{\partial y_j} = \frac{\partial E}{\partial x_j} \cdot \partial w_{ji} \qquad (A.8)$$

To compute the effect of all of the connections to unit $i$ we get:

$$\frac{\partial E}{\partial y_j} = \sum_i \frac{\partial E}{\partial x_j} \cdot \partial w_{ji} \qquad (A.9)$$

The final step is to change the weights by an amount proportional to the accumulated $\partial E/\partial w$:

$$\Delta w = -\varepsilon \frac{\partial E}{\partial w} \qquad (A.10)$$

The learning rate ($\varepsilon$) determines how much of the change in weights will be applied on each iteration. This approach will only be able to find the local minimum, as it will be unable to make changes in the weights that would have a temporary effect of increasing the error. In order to escape local minimums, a momentum factor can be introduced:

$$\Delta w(t+1) = -\varepsilon \frac{\partial E}{\partial w}(t+1) + \alpha \Delta w(t) \qquad (A.11)$$

The momentum term ($\alpha$) determines the degree of influence the previous weight change will have. We now have the equations needed for back-propagation.

To implement back-propagation on a three-layer, feed-forward neural net, the following algorithm can be used. The initialization for this algorithm requires the random initialization of all of the weight values and the setting of the learning rate ($\eta$) and the momentum term ($\alpha$).

* Loop until threshold is reached or maximum epochs exceeded
  do while tss > threshold and epoch < max_epochs

*       For each pattern
        for k = 1...P

*           Forward Pass — calculate outputs for hidden and
            output layers

$$h_j = \frac{1}{1 + e - \sum_{i=0}^{A} w1_{ij} x_i} \quad \text{for } j = 1 \ldots B$$

*           Backward pass — calculate errors

$$e2_j = y_j(1 - y_j)(d_j - y_j) \quad \text{for } j = 1 \ldots C$$

$$e1_j = h_j(1 - h_j) \sum_{i=1}^{C} e2_j w2_{ji} \quad \text{for } j = 1 \ldots B$$

*           Backward pass — adapt weight based on error

$$\Delta w2_{ij}(t+1) = \eta e2_j h_i + \alpha \Delta w2_{ij}(t)$$

$$\text{for } i = 0 \ldots B, j = 1 \ldots C$$

$$\Delta w1_{ij}(t+1) = \eta e1_j x_i + \alpha \Delta w1_{ij}(t)$$

$$\text{for } i = 0 \ldots A, j = 1 \ldots B$$

*           Compute pss

$$pss_k = \sum_{j=1}^{C} e2(k)_j^2$$

            endfor
*       Compute tss

$$tss = \sum_{k=1}^{P} pss_k$$

    endwhile

# References

Bailey, D., Thompson, D. (1990) Developing neural-network applications. *AI Expert*, Sep, 34–41.

Burke, G. (1993) Good trading a matter of breeding? *Futures*, May, 26–29.

Carpenter, W., Hoffman, M. (1995) Training backprop neural networks. *AI Expert*, Mar, 30–33.

Caudill, M. (1993)A little knowledge is a dangerous thing. *AI Expert*, Jun, 16–22.

Druey, K. (1995) Neural net input optimization. *Technical Analysis of Stocks and Commodities*, Dec, 69–75.

Felsen, J. (1990) Beating the market with an expert trading system. *Technical Analysis of Stocks and Commodities*, Dec, 47–52.

Fishman, M., Barr, D. (1991) A hybrid system for market timing. *Technical Analysis of Stocks and Commodities*, Aug, 26–34.

Fishman, M., Barr, D., Loick, W. (1991) Using neural nets in market analysis. *Technical Analysis of Stocks and Commodities*, Apr, 18–22.

Glazier, J. (1990) Archiving the experts. *Technical Analysis of Stocks and Commodities*, Jul, 38–42.

Hiotis, A. Inside a self-organizing map. *AI Expert*, Apr, 38–43.

Jurik, M. (1992) The care and feeding of a neural network. *Futures*, Oct, 40–44.

Knight, K. (1990) Connectionist ideas and algorithms. *Communications of the ACM*, **33**(11), 59–74.

Lippmann, R. (1987) An Introduction to computing with neural nets. *IEEE ASSP Magazine*, Apr, 4–22.

Lippmann, R. (1989) Pattern classification using neural networks. *IEEE Communications Magazine*, Nov, 47–64.

Lowe, D., Webb, A. (1991) Time series prediction by adaptive networks: a dynamical systems perspective. *IEE Proceedings-F*, **138**, 17–25.

Lung Shih, Y. (1991) Neural nets in technical analysis. *Technical Analysis of Stocks and Commodities*, Feb, 62–68.

Lupo, J. (1989) Defense Applications of Neural Networks. *IEEE Communications Magazine*, Nov, 82–88.

McClelland, J., Rumelhart, D. (1988) *Explorations in Parallel Distributed Processing: A Handbook of Models, Programs and Exercises*. MIT Press, Lancaster, MA.

Mendelsohn, L. (1991) The basics of developing a neural trading system. *Technical Analysis of Stocks and Commodities*, Jun, 54–56.

Murphy John, J. (1986) *Technical Analysis of the Futures Markets*. The New York Institute of Finance, Prentice Hall, New York.

Pardo, R. (1991) Walking forward can keep a trading model a step ahead. *Futures*,

Jul, 24–30.

Rogers, R., Vemuri, V. (1994) *Artificial Neural Networks Forecasting Time Series.* IEEE Computer Society Press, Los Alamitos, CA. © 1994, IEEE.

Ruggerio, M. (1994a) How to build an artificial trader. *Futures,* Sep 56–58.

Ruggerio, M. (1994b) Training neural nets for intermarket analysis. *Futures,* Aug, 42–44.

Ruggerio, M. (1995) Testing a real system. *Futures,* Apr, 46–48.

Rumelhart, D., Hinton, G., Williams, R. (1986) Learning representations by back-propagating errors. *Nature,* **323**, 533–536.

Stein, J. (1990) Man vs. machine: what trading style is best? *Futures,* Jul, 52–53.

Stein, J. (1991a) Neural networks: from the chalkboard to the trading room. *Futures,* May, 26–30.

Stein, J. (1991b) Expert systems enter gray area of gray matter. *Futures,* Aug, 16–18.

Tang, Z., de Alemeida, C., Fishwick, P. (1991) Time series forecasting using neural networks vs. Box-Jenkins methodology. *Simulation,* **57**, 303–310.

Versaggi, M. (1995) Understanding conflicting data. *AI Expert,* Apr, 21–25.

Wagner, G., Matheny, B. (1991) Pattern recognition and candlesticks. *Technical Analysis of Stocks and Commodities,* Sep, 74–79.

Ward, S., Sherald, M. (1995) The neural network financial wizards. *Technical Analysis of Stocks and Commodities,* Dec, 50–55.

Weigend, A., Rumelhart, D., Huberman, B. (1991) Generalization by weight-elimination with application to forecasting. *Advances in Neural Information Processing Systems,* **3**, 875–882.

# Index

# BrainTrader
# System Builder

## ORDER FORM

**BrainTrader System Builder (BTSB)** is a Windows application that implements many of the techniques found in this book. This software is to be released in 1996. BTSB includes feature extraction, data conversions, neural network simulations and walk-forward testing, all tailored for building a market trading system. If you are interested in more information on BTSB, please fill out the following form and mail it to the address indicated. You will be put on a mailing list and be notified when BTSB is available.

✁ - - - - - - - - - - - - - - - - - - - - - - - - - - - - - - - - ✁ - - - - - -

Name: _____

Address: _____

_____

City: _____   State/Zip: _____

Country: _____

*Mail to:*
MJ Futures
26 Birch Lane
Eatontown, New Jersey 07724
USA

✁ - - - - - - - - - - - - - - - - - - - - - - - - - - - - - - - - - - - - - -

MJ Futures is a commodity futures trading firm that provides software for trading and market analysis and trades personal accounts. MJ Futures also offers **NeuroGen**, a neural market development environment.